UNGLUED

Also by Lysa TerKeurst

Am I Messing Up My Kids?

Becoming More Than a Good Bible Study Girl

Becoming More Than a Good Bible Study Girl video curriculum

Capture His Heart (for wives)

Capture Her Heart (for husbands)

Leading Women to the Heart of God

Living Life on Purpose

Made to Crave

Made to Crave Devotional

Made to Crave for Teens

Made to Crave video curriculum

Made to Crave Action Plan video curriculum

Unglued

What Happens When Women Say Yes to God

What Happens When Women Say Yes to God video curriculum

What Happens When Women Walk in Faith

Who Holds the Key to Your Heart?

PARTICIPANT'S GUIDE
SIX SESSIONS

UNGLUED

MAKING WISE CHOICES
IN THE MIDST OF RAW EMOTIONS

NEW YORK TIMES BESTSELLING AUTHOR

LYSA TERKEURST

WITH CHRISTINE M. ANDERSON

ZONDERVAN®

ZONDERVAN.com/
AUTHORTRACKER
follow your favorite authors

ZONDERVAN

Unglued Participant's Guide
Copyright © 2012 by Lysa TerKeurst

This title is also available as a Zondervan ebook.
Visit www.zondervan.com/ebooks.

Requests for information should be addressed to:

Zondervan, *Grand Rapids, Michigan 49530*

ISBN 978-0-310-89215-1

Published in association with the literary agency of Fedd & Company, Inc., Post Office Box 341973, Austin, TX 78734.

Cover design: Curt Diepenhorst
Cover photography: Helena Inkera / Getty Images®
Interior design: Matthew Van Zomeren

Printed in the United States of America

14 15 16 17 18 /DCI/ 22 21 20 19 18 17 16 15 14 13 12 11 10 9

Contents

About the Study   7

How to Use This Guide   9

SESSION 1   Grace for the Unglued   11

SESSION 2   Freedom for the Unglued   41

SESSION 3   Four Kinds of Unglued   73

SESSION 4   A Procedure Manual for the Unglued   105

SESSION 5   Lingering Words for the Unglued   135

SESSION 6   Imperfect Progress for the Unglued   165

About the Study

Emotions aren't bad—I know this. But I also know what it's like to lie awake at night full of regret and disappointment because I couldn't control my reactions. So I vow to do better tomorrow, but better proves illusive and I fail again. Tears slip and I'm worn out from trying. Always trying.

Maybe you can relate. If you relate to my hurt, I pray you will also relate to my hope, found in a beautiful reality called *imperfect progress*. And that's the vision I am so excited to share with you in *Unglued*.

Just imagine what it might be like if you were able to …

- Face situations that are out of your control without acting out of control.
- Make it to the end of the day with no regrets from either spewing or stuffing emotions.
- Face almost any situation that bumps into your happy knowing you can handle yourself in a way that honors God.

That's the hope and the promise of imperfect progress—that God uses slow steps of progress wrapped in grace to lead us into lasting changes. As good as that sounds, it could be that it sounds a little too good to you. Or maybe you're not sure you want to even talk about your raw emotions, let alone immerse yourself in a study about how to address them. You might relate to one of these concerns …

- *My situation is too complex and difficult. A few Bible verses and inspirational sayings won't help me.* No matter how big or overwhelming the situation you're facing, there is power in being equipped with truth— emotional truth and God's truth. You can't control how other people act and react, but you can control how you act and react. And that's where there is potential for transformation, even in the most difficult circumstances.

- *This is just how I am.* When all we've really known is being angry or stuffing emotions, it's easy to believe labels like these are stamped on our souls with permanent ink. But God is bigger than any label and His truth can change you. It's changed me—and I really believe that if I can change, anyone can.

- *Even if change is possible, I'm too worn out to try again.* You're not alone. Isn't that good to know? There is a hurt we share. But I invite you to take a small step of risk and join me in drinking deeply from God's cup of hope and grace and peace. It is possible—you really can make progress starting right where you are.

My dear friend, will you join me in taking a closer look at raw emotions—and dare to believe that change is possible for you? It's okay if your progress is slow or you have to take a few steps back. Give yourself grace—progress wrapped in grace. We'll never be perfect until we get to heaven, but if we desire to grow a little more day by day, then year by year we will progress. And that's a beautiful thing!

I'd love to stay connected with you throughout your *Unglued* journey. Be sure to visit *www.Ungluedbook.com* where you'll find additional resources and encouragement. We can also connect on my blog, *www.LysaTerKeurst.com*. Stop by to tell me how you're doing. Plus, I'll keep posting new *Unglued* teachings even after the study is done.

Lysa TerKeurst

How to Use This Guide

Group Size

The *Unglued* video curriculum is designed to be experienced in a group setting such as a Bible study, Sunday school class, or any small group gathering. To ensure everyone has enough time to participate in discussions, it is recommended that large groups break up into smaller groups of four to six people each.

Materials Needed

Each participant should have her own participant's guide, which includes notes for video segments, activities, and discussion questions, as well as a reading plan and personal studies to deepen learning between sessions. Although the course can be fully experienced with just the video and participant's guide, participants are also encouraged to have a copy of the *Unglued* book. Reading the book along with the video sessions provides even deeper insights that make the journey richer and more meaningful.

What's Included

Unglued includes:

- Six group sessions
- Six days of personal study for use between each session. This includes suggested chapter readings from the *Unglued* book and personal Bible studies that track along with the book chapters and video teaching for group sessions.

Format Options

Unglued can be used by groups that meet for one hour or two hours. Each group session can be completed in one hour but includes optional activities and group discussions that expand the material to meet the needs of groups that meet for two hours.

Timing

The time notations —for example (17 minutes) —indicate the *actual* time of video segments and the *suggested* times for each activity or discussion. Adhering to the suggested times will enable you to complete each session in one hour. If you have additional time, you may wish to allow more time for discussion and activities.

Alternate time notations and optional activities for two-hour groups are set off with a gray background. For example:

The Crucial Question (15 MINUTES))

If your group meets for two hours, allow 25 minutes for this discussion.

In this example, one-hour groups allow 15 minutes for the discussion and two-hour groups allow 25 minutes for the discussion.

Facilitation

Each group should appoint a facilitator who is responsible for starting the video and for keeping track of time during discussions and activities. Facilitators may also read questions aloud and monitor discussions, prompting participants to respond and assuring that everyone has the opportunity to participate.

Personal Studies

Maximize the impact of the course between sessions with six days of personal study, alternating between Bible studies and reading chapters in the *Unglued* book. Setting aside twenty to thirty minutes a day for personal study will enable you to complete the book and Bible studies by the end of the six-week course.

SESSION

1

Grace for the Unglued

Welcome!

Welcome to Session 1 of *Unglued*. If this is your first time together as a group, take a moment to introduce yourselves to each other before watching the video. Then let's get started!

Video: *Grace for the Unglued* (18 MINUTES)

Play the video segment for Session 1. As you watch, use the outline (pages 11 – 13) to follow along or to take notes on anything that stands out to you.

Notes

Raw emotions — anger, frustration, bitterness, resentment — are the feelings we tend to hide from people we want to impress but spew on those we love the most.

Feelings should be indicators, not dictators.

Our goal in this study isn't to be perfect. Our goal is to make imperfect progress.

Joshua had to settle a crucial question (Joshua 6:1 – 5).

"Now when Joshua was near Jericho, he looked up and saw a man standing in front of him with a drawn sword in his hand. Joshua went up to him and asked, 'Are you for us or for our enemies?' " (Joshua 5:13).

Joshua is talking to the presence of God.

God's response to Joshua's question: "Neither" (Joshua 5:14a).

Joshua was asking the wrong question.

The crucial question Joshua needed to settle was, "Joshua, whose side are you on?"

Joshua settled that question and it gave him the courage to face his wall of impossibility.

We must settle this question as well. In our unglued situations, are we going to be on God's side or not?

How to remain on God's side:

"May the words of my mouth and the meditation of my heart be pleasing in your sight, O LORD, my Rock and my Redeemer" (Psalm 19:14, NIV 1984).

Ask yourself: What words am I speaking about this person? What thoughts am I having about this person?

1. Use truth.

2. Use self-control.

3. Use prayer.

Group Discussion

Video Debrief (5 MINUTES)

If your group meets for two hours, allow 10 minutes for this discussion.

1. What part of the video teaching had the most impact on you?

From Raw Reactions to Imperfect Progress (10 MINUTES)

If your group meets for two hours, allow 20 minutes for this discussion.

2. Which of the following animals best characterizes how you tend to respond when you are in an unglued situation? Share the reasons for your response.

☐ *Wounded bear*: I am hurt and unpredictable, so watch out.

☐ *Agitated skunk*: I may or may not create a stink, but the threat is always there.

☐ *Deceptive peacock*: Who me? I'm not upset. Look at all my pretty feathers!

☐ *Crouching tiger*: I may not attack now, but I will strike back when you least expect it.

☐ *Screech owl*: Prepare for a tirade!

☐ *Barricading beaver*: No time to say what I'm really feeling. I'm too busy building a wall between us.

☐ Other:

3. On the video, Lysa said that the goal of this study isn't to be perfect; the goal is to make *imperfect progress*—slow steps of change wrapped in grace.

• Generally speaking, what comes to mind when you think about trying to make a change? Examples: *I don't want this. Finally—something new! This is going to hurt. Change is bad. I'm excited to see what happens.*

• What was your initial response to Lysa's description of imperfect progress? How was your response similar to or different from the kind of thoughts you typically have when you think about change?

The Crucial Question (15 MINUTES)

If your group meets for two hours, allow 25 minutes for this discussion.

4. The book of Joshua is about conquering enemy territory. God's people have just emerged from forty years of desert wandering and are finally ready to claim the Promised Land as their own. After spying on the enemy (Joshua 2:1 – 3) and leading his own people to recommit themselves to God (Joshua 5:2 – 12), Joshua is on his way to survey the walls of Jericho in preparation for battle. But before he arrives, he discovers that a man he does not know is there ahead of him:

> Now when Joshua was near Jericho, he looked up and saw a man standing in front of him with a drawn sword in his hand. Joshua went up to him and asked, "Are you for us or for our enemies?"
>
> "Neither," he replied, "but as commander of the army of the LORD I have now come." Then Joshua fell facedown to the ground in reverence, and asked him, "What message does my Lord have for his servant?"
>
> The commander of the LORD's army replied, "Take off your sandals, for the place where you are standing is holy." And Joshua did so. (Joshua 5:13 – 15)

In this brief exchange, the commander of the Lord's army essentially says, "I'm not here to take sides. I'm here to take over."* Joshua, whom God has charged with taking possession of the land (Joshua 1:1 – 9), suddenly experiences a radical reorientation — about his role and about the battle he faces.

- How would you describe the shifts in Joshua's perspective — specifically, what do you think changes in how he sees his role and the battle he faces?

- Joshua's first question rebounds, forcing him to ask *himself* a crucial question: *Whose side am I on?* How does this question shift your perspective about your role in the battles you face, and about the battles themselves?

- What additional questions might this shift in perspective (or the story overall) stir up in you about your unglued experiences?

---

* "The Captain of the Lord's Army (Joshua 5:13 – 15)," J. Hampton Keathley, III, *www.bible.org* (accessed February 12, 2012).

Optional Group Discussion: *David's Impossible Battle* (20 MINUTES)

If your group meets for two hours, include this discussion as part of your meeting.

1. Read aloud portions of the David and Goliath story in 1 Samuel 17:4–11, 45–47. (If time permits, it's worthwhile to read all of chapter 17.)

2. How would you characterize the similarities and differences between Joshua's situation and David's situation?

3. God's work in Joshua's story is obvious and dramatic—the commander of the Lord's army appears to Joshua and gives clear instructions. How do you recognize God uniquely at work in David's story?

4. In what ways, if any, does David's story shift your perspective about your own impossible battles? For example, how does it help you to recognize how God might be at work in your difficulties? How does it help you understand what it might mean to find the courage you need to move ahead?

Choosing God's Side (15 MINUTES)

If your group meets for two hours, allow 25 minutes for this discussion.

5. Settling the crucial question—that he is on God's side—gives Joshua the courage he needs to face his wall of impossibility in a new way. We may not have all the answers when we find ourselves in an unglued moment, but we can use the prayer of the psalmist to shift our perspective and to position ourselves on God's side:

> May the words of my mouth and the meditation of my heart be pleasing in your sight, O LORD, my Rock and my Redeemer. (Psalm 19:14, NIV 1984)

- What image would you say best characterizes your words and your thoughts when you are in an unglued situation? For example: a runaway train, an underground nuclear explosion, an iceberg. Share the reasons for your response.

- Remake this same image to describe how you hope your words and thoughts might change if you could position yourself on God's side. For example: a runaway train might become a train slowly pulling into a station to offload cargo and refuel; an underground nuclear explosion might have an emergency "off" switch; an iceberg might melt into a spring-fed mountain lake.

- The psalmist uses the words *Rock* and *Redeemer* to describe his relationship to God. They are words that evoke images of protection and rescue. How do you need God to protect and rescue you in your unglued moments?

6. The five remaining sessions in the *Unglued* study explore many of the ways we come unglued and how we can use imperfect progress to make lasting changes. In addition to learning together as a group, it's important to be aware of how God is at work among you—especially in how you relate to each other and share your lives throughout the study. As you discuss the teaching in each session, there will be many opportunities to practice giving and receiving grace, to speak life-giving—and life-challenging—words, and to listen to one another deeply.

   Take a few moments to consider the kinds of things that are important to you in this setting. What do you need or want from the other members of the group? Use one or more of the sentence starters below, or your own statement, to help the group understand the best way to be a good companion to you throughout this *Unglued* journey. As each person responds, use the chart on pages 18 – 19 to briefly note what is important to that person and how you can be a good companion to her.

   It really helps me when ...

   I tend to withdraw or feel anxious when ...

   I'd like you to challenge me about ...

   I'll know this group is a safe place if you ...

   In our discussions, the best thing you could do for me is ...

NAME	THE BEST WAY I CAN BE A GOOD COMPANION TO THIS PERSON

NAME	THE BEST WAY I CAN BE A GOOD COMPANION TO THIS PERSON

Individual Activity: *What I Want to Remember* (2 MINUTES)

Complete this activity on your own.

1. Briefly review the outline and any notes you took.
2. In the space below, write down the most significant thing you gained in this session — from the teaching, activities, or discussions.

What I want to remember from this session . . .

Closing Prayer

Close your time together with prayer.

Between Now and the Next Session

Each session in *Unglued* includes a week's worth of personal studies to encourage you, prepare you for the next group discussion, and help you to make progress between meetings. In the studies this week, you'll have an opportunity each day to take "field notes" on your unglued experiences and to learn more about moving forward with grace — not guilt — as the foundation for lasting change.

Will you consider setting aside twenty to thirty minutes a day for grace-based personal study? It's an investment that promises to yield significant returns. Don't miss out!

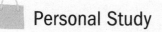

Personal Study

● DAY 1: **Study and Reflect**

> What kept me from making changes was the feeling I wouldn't do it perfectly. I knew I'd still mess up and the changes wouldn't come instantly.
>
> *Unglued*, page 14

1. The word pairings below describe a range of thoughts and emotions about change. Place an ✕ on each continuum to indicate how you tend to think and feel about the prospect of making changes in your life.

●————————————————————————————————●
Guilt   Grace

●————————————————————————————————●
Destination   Journey

●————————————————————————————————●
Small steps don't count   Everything counts

●————————————————————————————————●
Try hard   Train hard

●————————————————————————————————●
I don't want to   I am willing to want to

●————————————————————————————————●
Change is too hard   Not changing is harder

●————————————————————————————————●
Settling   Risking

●————————————————————————————————●
Comfort zone   Stretch zone

●————————————————————————————————●
Immediate results   Steady transition

Circle the continuum on which you placed the ✗ farthest to the left. How has this perspective kept you from making changes in the past?

Based on your responses on the continuums, how would you describe your current thoughts and feelings about change — especially in connection with your raw emotions and reactions?

2. God invites us to choose grace rather than self-condemnation — or anything else — as the starting point for growth and change. One of the most compelling illustrations of this truth comes from the Gospel story of the woman caught in adultery (John 8:1 – 11). After dispersing the crowd of accusers who wanted to stone her, Jesus addresses the woman directly:

> "Woman, where are they? Has no one condemned you?"
> "No one, sir," she said.
> "Then neither do I condemn you," Jesus declared. "Go now and leave your life of sin." (John 8:10 – 11)

There is nothing conditional about Jesus' response. He doesn't say, "If you promise to leave your life of sin, I won't condemn you." He first extends grace and then invites the woman to build a whole new life on that foundation. She doesn't change in order to receive Jesus' approval; she changes as a response to His love.

Take a moment to think about the changes you want to experience, especially in connection with your raw emotions and reactions. What intrigues you, or concerns you, about approaching these changes as a response to God's love?

Our goal isn't to be perfect; that's not realistic. Our goal is to make progress — imperfect progress.

Unglued DVD

---

3. Sometimes progress toward a goal is easy to measure. For example, when the goal is to eat healthy and lose weight, you might keep a food diary and step on a scale to establish your starting point (the "before" picture), and then do the same to periodically assess progress. Other times — as with raw reactions — progress can be a little more challenging to measure. That is why it's especially important to set a *goal* and know your *starting point*; if you don't know where you are or where you're going, it's really hard to measure progress!

My Goal

A goal is what you hope to accomplish stated in a way that is achievable and measurable. In connection with raw reactions, one way to think about a goal is to consider what you would like your new "normal" to be. For example:

I would like it to be normal that ...

> *I choose not to raise my voice when I am upset.*

> *I graciously acknowledge what I'm feeling rather than stuffing my emotions.*

> *I make it through a day without regretting how I treated someone.*

If you feel uncertain or resistant about writing down a goal, this is your first opportunity to extend yourself some grace! What you write down isn't forever written in cement; it's simply a way to get started — and you will have a chance to come back and adjust your goal later. So, with a healthy helping of grace, imagine what you might like your new normal to be. Then use the sentence starter below to describe your goal. (If you have a hard time settling on one statement, you may wish to first write down three or four and then circle the one that stands out most to you as your goal.)

I would like it to be normal that . . .

My Starting Point

Your starting point is what's true right now. The purpose of establishing a starting point is not to beat yourself up, but to provide a baseline for measuring progress. Since you can't step on a scale or take a "before" picture of raw emotions, you'll need to collect some field notes about yourself and your reactions this week. In the final study for this week, you'll use your notes to establish your starting point.

To start, use the questions on the chart (page 25) to make some observations about a recent unglued experience — a time when your emotions got the better of you. That could mean you expressed your emotions to someone else in a way you later regretted; or it might mean you stuffed your emotions and used them to beat yourself up. Whatever the case, keep your observations gentle. For now, you are simply noticing what happened.

PERSON	FIELD NOTES ON MY RAW REACTIONS 1. What was my physical and emotional state before the event? 2. What happened that prompted my raw reaction? 3. How did I react?
Example *Airport employee at the lost luggage counter*	1. *I was tired from staying up late the night before and stressed because my flight was delayed.* 2. *The woman behind the counter initially ignored me and then made me go look for my luggage on my own before doing anything to help me.* 3. *On the inside, I was boiling. On the outside, I used a tense tone of voice and short, staccato sentences to communicate how irritated I was.*

Throughout the week, set aside a few minutes of your reading and study time to repeat this same activity. Use the charts on pages 37 – 39 to briefly document your experiences. Some days there may be nothing to write down (a good day!) and other days there may be more than one (a grace day). The most important thing is to use gentle noticing and to gather observations you can use to establish your starting point.

Guided Prayer

Lord, thank You for Your unending grace for me. Today, especially I need Your tender mercies for . . .

Thank You for releasing me from the burden of my past mistakes and for loving me into the person You created me to be. Amen.

● DAY 2: **Read and Learn**

Use the charts on pages 37 – 39 to briefly document any observations about your emotions and reactions over the last twenty-four hours (see page 25 for guidance and examples).

Read chapter 1 of the *Unglued* book. Use the space below to note any insights or questions you want to bring to the next group session.

● DAY 3: **Study and Reflect**

Use the charts on pages 37 – 39 to briefly document any observations about your emotions and reactions over the last twenty-four hours (see page 25 for guidance and examples).

> Sometimes we girls think if we don't make instant progress, then real change isn't coming. But that's not so. There is a beautiful reality called imperfect progress. The day I realized the glorious hope of this kind of imperfect change is the day I gave myself permission to believe I really could be different.
>
> *Unglued*, page 14

1. Think about a few of your past efforts to make personal changes — for
    example, to pray more consistently, to make exercise a regular habit,
    to be more patient with your kids or a colleague, etc. Overall, how did
    you experience progress toward your goal? Circle the image below that
    best illustrates your response (or draw your own image in the space
    provided).

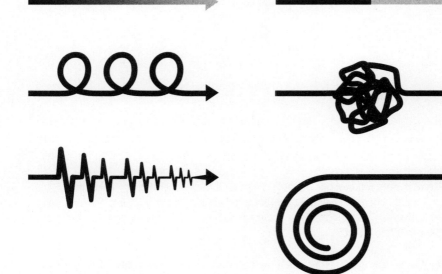

How do you relate the image you chose to your past experiences of progress toward change?

How might the image you chose represent imperfect progress?

2. The Bible uses several images that describe the process of growth and change. As you read about a few of those images below, underline any words or phrases that stand out to you.

> Good people will prosper like palm trees, and they will grow strong like the cedars of Lebanon. They will take root in your house, Lord God, and they will do well. They will be like trees that stay healthy and fruitful, even when they are old. (Psalm 92:12 – 14 CEV)

> And so we are transfigured much like the Messiah, our lives gradually becoming brighter and more beautiful as God enters our lives and we become like him. (2 Corinthians 3:18b MSG)

> Then Christ will make his home in your hearts as you trust in him. Your roots will grow down into God's love and keep you strong. (Ephesians 3:17 NLT)

> God is the one who began this good work in you, and I am certain that he won't stop before it is complete on the day that Christ Jesus returns. (Philippians 1:6 CEV)

What image stands out most to you? How is it similar to or different from the image you chose on page 27?

What do these passages reveal about the process of change?

How might these passages encourage you in connection with the changes you want to experience with your unglued emotions?

We won't bend from the weight of our past, but we will bow to the One who holds out hope for a better future. It's a truth-filled future in which God reveals how emotions can work for us instead of against us.

Unglued, page 17

Guided Prayer

Lord, thank You for releasing me from the weight of the past and for giving me hope that things really can be different.

Today, I especially need hope for . . .

Thank You for the promise that You have begun a good work in me, and that You won't stop until You complete it. That gives me hope! Amen.

● DAY 4: **Read and Learn**

Use the charts on pages 37–39 to briefly document any observations about your emotions and reactions over the last twenty-four hours (see page 25 for guidance and examples).

Read chapter 2 of *Unglued*. Use the space below to note any insights or questions you want to bring to the next group session.

● DAY 5: **Study and Reflect**

Use the charts on pages 37–39 to briefly document any observations about your emotions and reactions over the last twenty-four hours (see page 25 for guidance and examples).

> I can't control the things that happen to me each day, but I can control how I think about them. I can say to myself, "I have a choice to have destructive thoughts right now or constructive thoughts. I can wallow in what's wrong and make things worse or I can ask God for a better perspective to help me *see* good even when I don't *feel* good."
>
> *Unglued*, page 23

1. You may be familiar with the old folk tale about the six blind men who wanted to learn about elephants. As they all stand in different places around one of these huge creatures, each man reaches out to touch the animal and feel what it is like. To summarize:

   Touching its side, the first man describes the elephant as solid, like a wall. The second man touches the elephant's trunk and decides this creature is much like a snake. The tusk is what the third man encounters and he determines that the elephant is sharp, like a spear. Touching one of the animal's sturdy legs, the fourth man likens the elephant to a large cow. The fifth man runs his hand along the smooth flap of the elephant's ear and feels certain this creature can fly like a bird. The sixth man touches the animal's coarse tail and concludes that the elephant is nothing more than an old rope.

Every man's perspective on the elephant has some legitimacy, but each perspective is also severely limited. In every case, a limited perspective leads the men to wrong conclusions and keeps them from understanding the whole truth about the elephant.

When it comes to the unglued "elephants" in your own life, how do you relate, or not relate, to the blind men? For example, do you tend to think you have no blind spots and that you see the situation clearly? Do you generally resist or engage the challenge other perspectives pose to your own?

Identify a relationship in which you recently experienced an unglued moment (you may wish to refer to the names you wrote on the charts on pages 25, 37 – 39). Up until now, how would you assess the degree to which you have been tied to your own perspective about what happened? Check the box next to the word that best describes your response.

☐ *Minimally*

☐ *Fairly*

☐ *Moderately*

☐ *Considerably*

☐ *Entirely*

What thoughts or emotions are you aware of when you consider how this level of attachment to your perspective might have led you to wrong conclusions or prevented you from seeing a bigger truth — about yourself, this person, or what happened?

When faced with a situation out of our control, we need to ask, "Whose side am I on?" Will our response reflect that we are on God's side, or not? If we determine that, no matter what, we're on God's side, it settles the trust issue in our hearts. And if we ground ourselves in the reality that we trust God, we can face circumstances that are out of our control without acting out of control. We can't always fix our circumstances, but we can fix our minds on God. We can do that.

Unglued, page 28

2. Read the story of Joshua's encounter with the commander of the Lord's army in Joshua 5:13–15. Joshua's first question (verse 13) comes from what might be described as a "my way or the highway" perspective. But Joshua gets a whole new perspective when the commander essentially says, "I'm not here to take sides. I'm here to take over." This suddenly forces Joshua to come to grips with his own question: *Whose side am I on: God's side or my own?*

We choose God's side when we believe—really believe—that God is not only present in our circumstances but that He is also out to do us good. We believe it even when we can't feel it.

At the time, what made it difficult for you to trust that God was present in the situation you identified in question 1 (page 31)?

Looking back, are you now able to believe that God was present and out to do you good in this situation? If so, how do you recognize God at work? If not, what makes this difficult for you, or how do you hope God might be at work in ways you can't yet see?

Joshua could have resisted, but he chooses instead to rest; he surrenders his limited perspective and places his faith in God's perspective — even though he can't yet see it for himself.

How do you sense God may be inviting you to rest — in connection with this particular situation and in your emotional struggles overall?

I like the thought of impossible being erased from my vocabulary. Especially when it comes to my struggles with feeling unglued. I am on God's side. I can reflect that in my actions and reactions. I can face things out of my control without acting out of control.

Unglued, page 28

Guided Prayer

God, thank You for the liberating truth that nothing is impossible with You. Please erase impossible from my vocabulary, especially in connection with …

Today, I choose to be on Your side, trusting that You will help me to face things outside of my control without acting out of control. Amen.

● DAY 6: **Gentle Noticing:** *Establishing My Starting Point*

The Day 1 personal study provided an opportunity for you to identify a goal and to research your starting point by taking field notes on your raw emotions and reactions. If you weren't able to make notes during the week, do so now. Use the charts on pages 37 – 39 to describe two or three raw emotions or reactions you experienced this week. If you can't recall anything from this week, write down any recent experiences you can think of. For guidance and examples, see page 25.

1. Briefly review what you wrote on your charts (pages 25, 37 – 39). What common issues or behaviors do you recognize in the following areas?

   The frequency of my raw emotions/reactions …

   Example: Two to three times a week

   The people who prompt my raw emotions/reactions …

   Example: My kids are almost always the ones who prompt my unglued reactions.

   My physical and emotional state before the events …

   Example: Most of the time I am tired, hurried, and worried about something.

What happened that prompted my raw emotions/reactions . . .

Example: The kids typically say or do something that makes life harder for me, embarrasses me, or prevents me from doing something I need to do. And it usually feels like they're standing on the last good nerve I have left.

How I reacted . . .

Example: Most of the time I yell. Sometimes I slam doors or march around the house giving orders or lectures. Later, I almost always end up stewing in a vat of guilt and regret.

Additional observations . . .

2. A starting point is what's true right now; it provides a baseline for measuring progress. Drawing on your responses from question 1, briefly summarize your unglued behaviors. This is your starting point.

   Example: Two to three times a week, I yell at my kids and physically demonstrate my frustration by slamming doors. Then I feel guilty and beat myself up about it.

3. Turn to page 24 and review the "new normal" you wrote down. Having established your starting point, does the statement on page 24 still accurately reflect the change you hope to experience? Make any necessary adjustments and then write down the new normal you hope for. This is your goal.

   Example: I would like it to be normal that I express my frustrations and discipline my kids without yelling or slamming doors.

Guided Prayer

God, thank You for loving me right where I am — and for loving me so much that You don't want me to get stuck here.

You know my heart and all my tangled-up thoughts and emotions. Right now, I am most concerned about . . .

Lord, I commit my starting place and my goal to You. I choose to trust that Your grace and Your mercies will be new for me each day. Please don't let me down! Amen.

PERSON	FIELD NOTES ON MY RAW REACTIONS
	1. What was my physical and emotional state before the event? 2. What happened that prompted my raw reaction? 3. How did I react?

PERSON	FIELD NOTES ON MY RAW REACTIONS 1. What was my physical and emotional state before the event? 2. What happened that prompted my raw reaction? 3. How did I react?

PERSON	FIELD NOTES ON MY RAW REACTIONS 1. What was my physical and emotional state before the event? 2. What happened that prompted my raw reaction? 3. How did I react?

Freedom for the Unglued

Group Discussion: *Checking In* (5 MINUTES)

If your group meets for two hours, allow 10 minutes for this discussion.

Welcome to Session 2 of *Unglued*. A key part of getting to know God better is sharing your journey with others. Before watching the video, briefly check in with each other about your experiences since the last session. For example:

- What insights did you discover in the personal study or in the chapters you read from the *Unglued* book?
- How did the last session impact your daily life or your relationship with God?
- What questions would you like to ask the other members of your group?

Video: *Freedom for the Unglued* (15 MINUTES)

Play the video segment for Session 2. As you watch, use the outline (pages 41 – 44) to follow along or to take notes on anything that stands out to you.

Notes

Michelangelo's incomplete sculptures are called *Prisoners*.

These sculptures could be me — a prisoner locked away in hard places. These are the places I need to be chiseled. It's beautiful when the Master chisels.

Instead of condemning myself with statements like, "I'm such a mess," I can say, "Let God chisel."

God chisels us, but He never leaves us during the chiseling process. We are God's workmanship, His masterpiece.

"As you come to him, the living Stone — rejected by humans but chosen by God and precious to him — you also, like living stones, are being built into a spiritual house to be a holy priesthood, offering spiritual sacrifices acceptable to God through Jesus Christ. . . . But you are a chosen people, a royal priesthood, a holy nation, God's special possession, that you may declare the praises of him who called you out of darkness into his wonderful light" (1 Peter 2:4 – 5, 9).

Peter's name means "the rock," but his given name was Simon, which means "shifty." Peter didn't get stuck being shifty his whole life because he let God chisel.

Jesus saw Peter not as he was, but as he could be. Tenderly, Jesus chiseled.

Jesus set a true scene of grace for Peter. We get to see Jesus chiseling (John 21:15 – 17).

We see evidence of the chiseled Peter in Acts 2.

"For we are God's workmanship, created in Christ Jesus to do good works, which God prepared in advance for us to do" (Ephesians 2:10 NIV 1984).

God is chiseling us, releasing us from our hard places so we can do good works.

"For it is by grace you have been saved, through faith — and this not from yourselves, it is the gift of God — not by works, so that no one can boast" (Ephesians 2:8 – 9 NIV 1984).

This week, as hard things happen, practice pausing before reacting and whisper, "Let God chisel."

Group Discussion

Video Debrief (5 MINUTES)

If your group meets for two hours, allow 10 minutes for this discussion.

1. What part of the video teaching had the most impact on you?

The Prisoners (7 MINUTES)

If your group meets for two hours, allow 15 minutes for this discussion.

2. Lysa contrasted Michelangelo's unfinished sculptures called *Prisoners* with his masterpiece *David* to illustrate the difference between a soul stuck in hard places and a soul chiseled into a masterpiece by God.

   In what ways do you relate to each image on page 45? For example, how does the unfinished sculpture represent something true about you and the state of your soul? How might the *David* sculpture represent chiseling God has already completed in you, or perhaps represent something you desire to be true in your life with God?

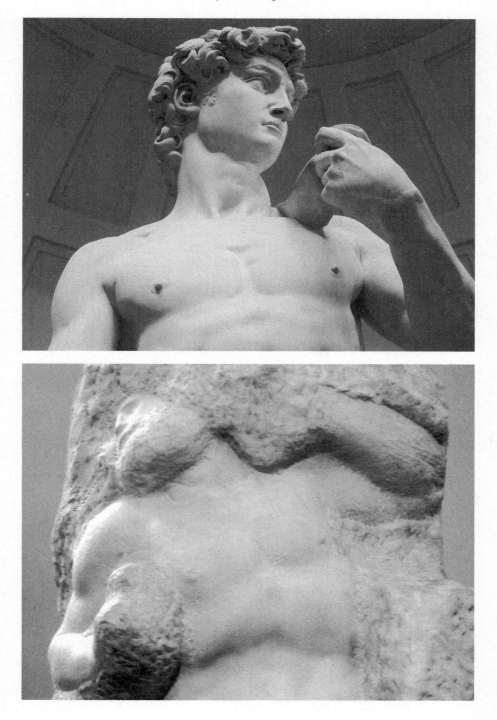

Let God Chisel (10 MINUTES)

If your group meets for two hours, allow 25 minutes for this discussion.

3. When asked how he had completed the David statue, Michelangelo is reported to have said, "It was easy. I just chipped away the stone that didn't look like David." God is inclined to say something similar to us: *I want to chip away the things that don't look like you. And these unglued moments and failures? They don't look like you.*

   How are you challenged or encouraged to consider that this is how God sees you and your struggles?

4. God doesn't allow the unglued moments of our lives to happen so that we'll label ourselves and stay stuck. He allows the unglued moments to make us aware of the chiseling that needs to be done.

   • Briefly describe a recent raw emotion or unglued experience. What kinds of self-defeating thoughts or labels ran through your head in the aftermath of that experience?

   • Beyond the experience itself, what underlying issues does your reaction make you aware of?

   • On the video, Lysa says, "Instead of condemning myself, I can say, 'Let God chisel.'" What do you think this might mean for you in practical terms? In other words, what changes in behavior, thinking, or spiritual practices would enable you to "let God chisel"?

Grace Is Required (17 MINUTES)

If your group meets for two hours, allow 30 minutes for this discussion.

5. God is chiseling us, making us new. Like Michelangelo's *David*, we are God's creation—His masterpiece. Here is how the apostle Paul describes it:

> For we are God's *workmanship*, created in Christ Jesus to do good works, which God prepared in advance for us to do. (Ephesians 2:10 NIV 1984, emphasis added)

The Greek word translated here as "workmanship" is *poiema* (poy'-ay-mah). In literal translation it means "what is made, work, creation."* As a noun, workmanship can refer to either the *object* an artisan creates or to the *skill and activity* of the artisan. In the preceding verses, Paul states the spiritual foundation for God's workmanship:

> For it is by *grace* you have been saved, through faith—and this not from yourselves, it is the gift of God—not by works, so that no one can boast. (Ephesians 2:8–9 NIV 1984, emphasis added)

- How does Paul's image of God as an artisan or master craftsman impact your view of God and His work in you? How does it compare to other images you might have of God, such as a father or a judge?

- Based on the Ephesians verses and what you've learned about Michelangelo's sculptures, how would you describe what it means to be a work in process? For example, what do you imagine Michelangelo needed and expected from his blocks of marble? What parallels might you draw between Michelangelo's raw material and the raw material of your own life?

---

* Friedrich Thiele, *"poiema," New International Dictionary of New Testament Theology*, vol. 3, Colin Brown, gen. ed. (Grand Rapids: Zondervan, 1978, 1986), 1152.

- Sculpting a masterpiece doesn't happen overnight—it's a process that requires time and careful work. The same is true for imperfect progress. God is chiseling us, making us new—and that requires time, careful work, and a great deal of grace. Where do you feel grace is most lacking, either in your life with God overall or specifically in your struggles with raw emotions? What grace do you need from God right now?

Optional Partner Activity: *More Than Grace* (20 MINUTES)

If your group meets for two hours, include this activity as part of your meeting.

1. Pair up with one other person.
2. Listed below are several "grace and" statements from Scripture. Taking turns, read through the list out loud.

> For the LORD God is our sun and our shield. He gives us *grace and glory [honor]*. The LORD will withhold no good thing from those who do what is right. (Psalm 84:11 NLT, emphasis added)

> For the law was given through Moses; *grace and truth* came through Jesus Christ. (John 1:17, emphasis added)

> By God's *grace and mighty power*, I have been given the privilege of serving him by spreading this Good News. (Ephesians 3:7 NLT, emphasis added)

> But grow in the *grace and knowledge* of our Lord and Savior Jesus Christ. To him be glory both now and forever! Amen. (2 Peter 3:18, emphasis added)

> *Grace, mercy, and peace*, which come from God the Father and from Jesus Christ—the Son of the Father—will continue to be with us who live in truth and love. (2 John 1:3 NLT, emphasis added)

3. Which of the "grace and" phrases from Scripture would you use to complete this sentence: *In my struggles with raw emotions, I especially need grace and* _____ *right now.*

4. What insights or connections might you make between the verse that contains your "grace and" phrase and what you need right now? For example, if your phrase is "grace and mercy," from 2 John 1:3, what insights does this verse as a whole provide about mercy or how you might experience mercy?

5. One of the Bible's most frequently used "grace and" phrases is *grace and peace*. It is among the most common blessings the apostle Paul uses to greet his readers (Romans 1:12; 1 Corinthians 1:3; 2 Corinthians 1:2; Philippians 1:2; Galatians 1:3; Ephesians 1:2; 2 Thessalonians 1:2). At first glance, the words *grace* and *peace* might seem to be very similar, perhaps even redundant. But Paul's repeated use of these words in combination suggests that (1) each makes a unique and essential contribution, and (2) together, they are even more powerful in the life of a believer.

Briefly review the following two lists of words that describe grace and peace.

Grace	Peace
Love	Harmony
Mercy	Calm
Favor	Stillness
Goodwill	Quiet
Kindness	Silence
Blessing	Freedom from disturbance
Generosity of spirit	Lack of anxiety
Forgiveness	Serenity
Freedom from sin	Absence of conflict
Accommodation	Acceptance
Elegance	Contentment
Beauty	Rest

• Using the two lists as a reference, consider the unique and essential contributions of both grace and peace. How would your relationship with God and your experience of faith be different if you could have only one or the other? For example, grace but no peace, or peace but no grace.

• How would you describe the collaboration between grace and peace? For example, how do grace and peace increase, strengthen, and balance each other in the life of the believer?

• Identify one word or phrase in each list that stands out most to you. What connections might you make between these words? For example, if you chose *kindness* and *rest*, how do kindness and rest relate to each other or reinforce each other? How do you currently experience, or want to experience, both things in your relationship with God?

6. At the end of the group discussion for Session 1, you had the opportunity to share what you need from the other members of the group and to write down the best ways you can be good companions to one another (pages 18–19).

- Briefly restate what you asked for from the group in Session 1. What additions or clarifications would you like to make that would help the group know more about how to be a good companion to you? As each person responds, add any additional information to the chart on pages 18–19. (If you were absent from the last session, share your response to question 6 on page 17. Then use the chart to write down what is important to each member of the group.)

- In what ways, if any, did you find yourself responding differently to other members of the group in this session based on what they asked for in the previous session? What made that easy or difficult for you to do?

Individual Activity: *What I Want to Remember* (2 MINUTES)

Complete this activity on your own.

1. Briefly review the outline and any notes you took.

2. In the space below, write down the most significant thing you gained in this session — from the teaching, activities, or discussions.

What I want to remember from this session . . .

Closing Prayer

Close your time together with prayer.

Between Now and the Next Session

In the upcoming personal studies, you'll have an opportunity to continue taking field notes on your unglued experiences. The focus this week is on overcoming self-defeating labels and exploring four kinds of unglued reactions. The invitation each day is to embrace the hope of imperfect progress and to continue learning more about moving forward with grace — not guilt — as the foundation for lasting change.

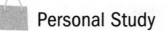

Personal Study

● DAY 1: **Study and Reflect**

> I was an inmate in a prison of my own design and locked behind the many, many labels I'd put on myself over the years. I'd resigned myself to the lie that I would forever be enslaved to my emotions. And I spoke to myself in ways I'd never let another person speak to me.
>
> *Unglued*, page 34

1. Over time, negative thought patterns can become self-defeating labels that impact how we see ourselves and keep us stuck in hard places. Instead of seeing our failures as temporary setbacks, we begin to see them as permanent conditions or even as part of our identity. We think things like . . .

   I always mess up.   *I'm such a coward.*
   Things will never get better. *I'm just like my parents.*
   I'll never lose weight.   *I'll always be a screamer.*

   Briefly reflect on the simplified image of a *Prisoners* sculpture (below) and how it might symbolize the labels and thought patterns that keep you stuck. What self-condemning labels come to mind when you think about your raw emotions and reactions? On or around the image, write down four to six of these labels.

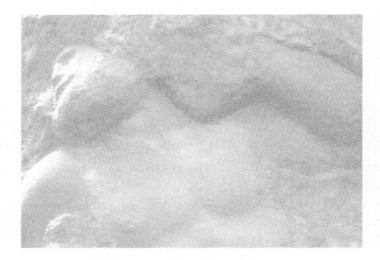

2. Briefly review the labels you wrote on the *Prisoners* image. Circle two that stand out most to you and write them in the left column on the chart below. Use the two remaining columns to briefly reflect on the impact these labels have on how you see yourself and how they keep you stuck.

SELF-DEFEATING LABELS	THE IMPACT THIS LABEL HAS HAD ON HOW I SEE MYSELF	HOW THIS LABEL KEEPS ME STUCK
Example: I always mess up.	I tend to think of myself as flawed and prone to failure. On those rare occasions when I don't mess up, I consider it a fluke.	It's difficult for me to hope that I can change and make progress, so I either don't try or I give up at the first setback.

3. Like us, the apostle Peter was someone whose emotions kept him stuck in hard places. Here are just a few examples of his raw reactions:

   • Peter dares to jump out of a boat and walk on water to Jesus, but then becomes terrified and begins to sink (Matthew 14:22 – 32).

   • Peter actually tries to rebuke Jesus for predicting His own suffering and death. In turn, Jesus strongly rebukes Peter, saying, "Get away from me, Satan!" (Matthew 16:21 – 23).

- Peter draws his sword in anger and cuts off the ear of a man named
  Malchus, a servant of the high priest who was among those who came to
  arrest Jesus in Gethsemane (John 18:1–10).
- After Jesus is arrested, Peter's fears cause him to deny Jesus three times
  (John 18:15–18, 25–27).

Choose one of these examples and read the indicated passage in your
Bible.

What self-defeating labels do you imagine Peter might have attached
to himself after this experience?

In what ways, if any, do you relate to Peter's raw reaction and to the labels
you identified?

4. The name Peter means "rock," but Peter's given name was Simon, which
   means "shifty." According to John's gospel, the first thing Jesus does
   when He meets Simon is rename him:

   Jesus looked at him and said, "You are Simon son of John. You will be called
   Cephas" (which, when translated, is Peter). (John 1:42)

   It is interesting to note that Jesus renames Simon *before* chiseling away
   his rough edges. At this point, Simon Peter's character was still a lot like
   one of Michelangelo's unfinished sculptures — stuck in hard places and
   trapped by weaknesses and raw reactions. But Jesus gives him a new
   name that reflects a deeper truth about Simon Peter's identity.

   Read John 1:35–42 for the full account of how Simon Peter meets
   Jesus. As you read, use your five senses to imagine the scenes in the
   narrative — what do you see, hear, smell, taste, and touch? Then put
   yourself in Simon's place. You are meeting Jesus for the first time and you
   hear Him say something like this: *I see you. I know who you are right now,
   and I know the deeper truth about who you really are.*

What thoughts or emotions come to mind as you imagine Jesus speaking these words to you?

I see you . . .

I know who you are right now . . .

I know the deeper truth about who you really are . . .

Guided Prayer

Lord, thank You for seeing me. I am so grateful that You know me even better than I know myself.

I am struggling right now with some self-defeating labels. I especially feel stuck with . . .

God, soften my heart. I know I need to surrender who I am right now so You can chisel me into my true self, the person You made me to be. Amen.

The Week Ahead

As part of the Session 1 personal studies, you had a chance to take daily field notes on your raw reactions. This week, you'll use the charts on pages 70–72 to continue taking field notes as you did before, but now with one additional question: *What words or phrases did I use to mentally label myself afterward?*

Allow a few minutes of your reading and study time each day to briefly document your experiences. Remember that the purpose of writing things down is not to beat yourself up, but to raise awareness and to begin measuring (imperfect) progress.

● DAY 2: **Read and Learn**

Use the charts on pages 70–72 to briefly document any observations about your emotions and reactions over the last twenty-four hours (see page 25 for guidance and examples).

Read chapter 3 of the *Unglued* book. Use the space below to note any insights or questions you want to bring to the next group session.

● DAY 3: **Study and Reflect**

Use the charts on pages 70–72 to briefly document any observations about your emotions and reactions over the last twenty-four hours (see page 25 for guidance and examples).

> I recognized a truth I'd needed to see for a long, long time: It is beautiful when the Master chisels.... Instead of condemning myself with statements like, *I'm such a mess,* I could say, *Let God chisel. Let Him work on my hard places so I can leave the dark places of being stuck and come into the light of who He designed me to be.* God is calling us out—out of darkness, out from those places we think will never get better—out of being stuck.
>
> *Unglued,* pages 36–37

1. Read the personal story Lysa shares in "Grace over Labels" on page 58. Then use the process Lysa describes to work through one of the self-defeating labels you're struggling with.

   I identified the label as a lie meant to tear me down. Write down a label that keeps you stuck (you may wish to choose one of the labels you wrote on the chart on page 52). What are the reality, the lie, and the truth about this label?

   A label that keeps me stuck:

   The reality about this label:

   The lie about this label:

   The truth about this label:

I chose to view this circumstance as a call to action, not a call to beat myself up mentally. What actions, however small, might you take to address the difficult situations or issues that lead you to label yourself? For now, focus on brainstorming three to five potential actions. Later, you can review your options and choose which actions to follow through on.

I used the momentum of tackling one label to help me tackle more. Tackling labels is like a good workout—it builds spiritual and emotional strength. What specific strengths do you hope this process of tackling labels might build in you?

Grace over Labels

I was locked behind the many, many labels I'd put on myself over the years. I'd resigned myself to the lie that I would forever be enslaved to my emotions....

Take my struggle with organization. For months, my messy closet was a source of mental contention. Every day I walked in and out of this space thinking, *Uggghh! Why am I so disorganized? Why can't I have a closet like so-and-so? I don't think she ever struggles with keeping things tidy. I'm just a mess.*

I labeled myself as a mess and then resigned myself to forever being a mess....

When I defined myself as a mess, my emotions felt even messier. I was more short-tempered and off-kilter. As I untangled the root of what was making me feel this way, I did three things:

I identified the label as a lie meant to tear me down.

The reality: My closet was messy. The lie: A messy closet means I am a mess. The truth: A messy closet does not make me a mess. It makes me a child of God who has a messy closet.

Grace. I can see it. I can feel it. I can call it grace.

I chose to view this circumstance as a call to action, not a call to beat myself up mentally.

A messy closet means I need to hit the pause button on life one day and clean it. And if I can't figure out how to clean it, then I need to find someone gifted in this area to help me. And that's exactly what I did. My friend Lisa has the spiritual gift of closet organization. (Is there such a thing?) I saved up my pennies and paid her to come and share some of that Jesus-equipping with me.

Grace. I can see it. I can feel it. I can call it grace.

I used the momentum of tackling one label to help me tackle more.

Taking action and tearing down this one label in my life has given me the courage to tackle other labels. Oh, the courage and strength found in starting somewhere! Might you find a small label to tackle today?

Grace. You will see it. You will feel it. You will call it grace.

Unglued, pages 34, 40

2. Throughout her three-step process, Lysa emphasizes grace. We tend to think of grace as an expression of God's mercy and forgiveness, but grace is also an expression of God's power. The apostle Paul acknowledges this power in Romans 5:20b. As you read through the four versions of this verse below, underline any words or phrases that stand out to you.

> Where sin increased, grace increased all the more. (NIV)

> Where sin was powerful, God's kindness was even more powerful. (CEV)

> Where sin increased and abounded, grace (God's unmerited favor) has surpassed it and increased the more and superabounded. (AMP)

> Sin didn't, and doesn't, have a chance in competition with the aggressive forgiveness we call grace. When it's sin versus grace, grace wins hands down. (MSG)

What connections do you make between the words and phrases you underlined and your need for grace with your raw emotions and reactions?

In what ways are you experiencing, or wanting to experience, God's grace as power? In other words, how are experiences of God's kindness giving you strength, confidence, or hope?

Let God chisel. "Trust me," God says, "it will be beautiful. You'll see."
Unglued, page 41

3. The chiseling process is about subtraction rather than addition. To grow in holiness and grace, we stand in God's loving presence and agree to let go of anything He wants to chip away.

How do you feel about your chiseling process right now? For example, are you able to experience God as a loving presence in this area of your life? To what degree are you able to let go and trust God?

Briefly review the list of actions you wrote down on page 57. Is there an option that feels like a graced invitation to let go and trust God? If so, write it below. If not, in what other way do you sense God may be inviting you to let go and trust Him?

Guided Prayer

God, where would I be without Your grace? Thank You for Your relentless love and all the ways Your grace gives me strength.

I know the chiseling process is what I need, but it's also hard for me. I especially need Your help to let go of . . .

I trust in Your love for me, Lord. I believe that every clink of Your divine chiseling brings me closer to freedom, closer to my true identity, and closer to You. Amen.

● DAY 4: **Read and Learn**

Use the charts on pages 70–72 to briefly document any observations about your emotions and reactions over the last twenty-four hours (see page 25 for guidance and examples).

Read chapter 4 of the *Unglued* book. Use the space below to note any insights or questions you want to bring to the next group session.

● DAY 5: **Study and Reflect**

Use the charts on pages 70–72 to briefly document any observations about your emotions and reactions over the last twenty-four hours (see page 25 for guidance and examples).

> Exploding means pushing emotions outward.... The telltale sign of being an exploder is not the decibel level but having a reaction that feels good in the moment because it gets the yuck out....
>
> Stuffing means pushing emotions inward. We swallow hard and lock our hurt feelings inside, not in an effort to process and release them, but to wallow in the hurt.
>
> *Unglued*, page 44

1. Briefly review your field notes so far (pages 37–39, 70–72). For each experience you wrote down, assess whether your reaction was characterized more by exploding (pushing emotions outward) or by stuffing (pushing emotions inward). In the margin, write "E" next to exploding reactions and "S" next to stuffing reactions.

When you are stressed, irritated, stuck in conflict, hurt, or causing hurt, do your reactions tend more toward stuffing or exploding? Place an ✗ on the continuum to indicate your unglued tendency.

●——●

Stuffing
I tend to push my
emotions inward.

Exploding
I tend to push my
emotions outward.

How would you describe the "benefits" of your unglued tendency? In other words, how does your tendency give you something you need in the short term? For example: *it gets the yuck out, keeps the peace, buys me time, gives me a sense of power when I feel powerless, helps me to feel protected, makes me look more spiritual,* etc.

I determined that there are ... four categories of unglued reactions:

- · Exploders who shame themselves
- · Exploders who blame others
- · Stuffers who build barriers
- · Stuffers who collect retaliation rocks

Can you see yourself in any of these? I can.... I realized I fall into all four categories!

Depending on the situation and the people involved, I shift my unglued reactions. I know I will pay a cost for coming unglued. Somehow, I instinctively measure this cost and decide with whom and in what circumstances I can afford to either explode and let it all rip, or stuff it and pretend nothing is wrong.

Unglued, page 45

---

2. Read through the descriptions of the four kinds of unglued reactions in the left columns of the charts on pages 63 and 64. Then use the right columns on the charts to reflect on how you may have experienced each kind of reaction.

EXPLODERS	
Exploders push emotions outward. Behaviors might include stern words; harsh looks; condemning attitudes; possibly, but not necessarily, a raised voice or demonstrative gestures.	
TWO KINDS OF EXPLODERS	**HOW I HAVE EXPERIENCED EXPLODING** With whom do I typically react this way? What circumstances tend to provoke this kind of reaction in me? What behaviors characterize my reactions? What short-term benefits do I get from this reaction?
EXPLODERS WHO SHAME THEMSELVES I process hurt or aggravation by releasing my emotions on others and then use self-condemning thoughts to deal with my regret.	
EXPLODERS WHO BLAME OTHERS I process hurt or aggravation by releasing my emotions on others and then blame others for provoking my reactions in order to deal with my regret.	

NOTE: For additional guidance in assessing your unglued reactions, see the appendix in the *Unglued* book, pages 193–197.

STUFFERS	
Stuffers push emotions inward. Behaviors might include swallowing hurt feelings; saying everything is fine when it's not; keeping a mental record of wrongs; denying negative emotions such as anger, hurt, or disappointment; wallowing in negative emotions.	
TWO KINDS OF STUFFERS	**HOW I HAVE EXPERIENCED STUFFING** With whom do I typically react this way? What circumstances tend to provoke this kind of reaction in me? What behaviors characterize my reactions? What short-term benefits do I get from this reaction?
STUFFERS WHO BUILD BARRIERS I process hurt or aggravation by denying it in the moment and then withdrawing behind an emotional barrier that shuts down communication.	
STUFFERS WHO COLLECT RETALIATION ROCKS I process hurt or aggravation by denying it in the moment while keeping a mental record of wrongs I can use later as proof against the other person.	

NOTE: For additional guidance in assessing your unglued reactions, see the appendix in the *Unglued* book, pages 193–197.

There is nothing wrong with having feelings. Feelings are good. God made us to be emotional creatures who experience the highs and lows of life through our feelings. But while feelings are great indicators of what we are experiencing, they shouldn't dictate how we react to our circumstances. Feelings should be indicators, not dictators.

Unglued DVD

3. When emotions dictate our reactions—exploding or stuffing—we're all too familiar with the regret and hurt that follow. However, we sometimes neglect to consider the "indicators" hidden in these same emotions. Indicators often represent legitimate human needs. For example: the need to be heard or understood; to have a choice in what happens to us; to express hurt or confusion; to be loved and cared for.

When you consider your recent unglued reactions, how would you describe your indicators—the legitimate human needs hidden in your reactions?

What connections do you make between the legitimate human needs you identified and your relationship with God? For example, how might the things you need from other people also be indicators of things you need from God?

Guided Prayer

God, thank You for giving me emotions. Even though mine sometimes feel like a burden rather than a blessing, I know that having emotions is part of what it means to be made in Your image.

When I consider how my emotions are indicators, I get a clearer understanding of what I need and want — from my relationships and from You. Right now, I am especially aware of my needs for . . .

Thank You for the promise that You have already given me everything I need to live a godly life (2 Peter 1:3). Please help me to rely on this promise today. Amen.

● DAY 6: **Gentle Noticing**

The personal studies this week provided an opportunity for you to continue taking field notes on your raw emotions and reactions. If you weren't able to make notes during the week, do so now. Use the charts on pages 70–72 to describe two or three raw emotions or reactions you experienced this week. For guidance and examples, see page 25.

1. Briefly review two things: (1) what you wrote on your charts this week (pages 70–72), and (2) what you wrote in response to question 1 from last week's Day 6 study (pages 34–35). What similarities or differences do you notice between last week and this week in the following areas?

   The frequency of my raw emotions/reactions this week compared to last week . . .

   Example: About the same — two to three times a week.

The people who prompt my raw emotions/reactions this week compared to last week . . .

Example: My kids are still the ones who usually prompt my raw reactions, but I also noticed that I have more reactions to my coworkers than I thought—I just tend to stuff those feelings rather than express them.

My physical and emotional state before the events of this week compared to last week . . .

Example: Being tired was a bigger factor this week than it was last week.

What happened that prompted my raw emotions/reactions this week compared to last week . . .

Example: The kids seemed to make a point of being late every day this week, which made me angry with them—and also made me late to work.

When one of my coworkers innocently asked about a deadline in a meeting, I was embarrassed because I had to admit I was behind on the project. Then I felt angry because I thought he was judging me in front of everyone about being late to work.

How I reacted this week compared to last week . . .

Example: I did yell at the kids and lecture them, but I didn't slam any doors this week. Progress!

With my coworker, I didn't yell and I tried to hide my anger. But all day long I couldn't stop thinking about how he embarrassed me in the meeting. I spent the rest of the day trying to avoid him and didn't respond to any of his emails.

The words and phrases I used to label myself afterward . . .

Example: I'm such a bad mom. My kids probably tell all their friends how mean I am.

I'm always angry. I'm a bad person and a spiritual failure.

Additional observations about this week compared to last week . . .

2. How did you experience God at work in you this week? For example: in experiences of grace, gentle chiseling, or imperfect progress?

Guided Prayer

God, thank You for all the ways You are at work in me. Even though I can't always see it, I trust Your workmanship in me.

Today, I ask You to open my eyes so I can recognize Your presence in my life. I especially need to know You are at work in . . .

I entrust myself and my imperfect progress to You. Thank You for giving me the grace I need to see myself more clearly and to recognize Your chiseling work in me. Amen.

PERSON	FIELD NOTES ON MY RAW REACTIONS
	1. What was my physical and emotional state before the event?
	2. What happened that prompted my raw reaction?
	3. How did I react?
	4. What words or phrases did I use to mentally label myself afterward?

PERSON	FIELD NOTES ON MY RAW REACTIONS
	1. What was my physical and emotional state before the event? 2. What happened that prompted my raw reaction? 3. How did I react? 4. What words or phrases did I use to mentally label myself afterward?

PERSON	FIELD NOTES ON MY RAW REACTIONS 1. What was my physical and emotional state before the event? 2. What happened that prompted my raw reaction? 3. How did I react? 4. What words or phrases did I use to mentally label myself afterward?

SESSION

3

Four Kinds of Unglued

Group Discussion: *Checking In* (5 MINUTES)

If your group meets for two hours, allow 10 minutes for this discussion.

Welcome to Session 3 of *Unglued*. A key part of getting to know God better is sharing your journey with others. Before watching the video, briefly check in with each other about your experiences since the last session. For example:

- What insights did you discover in the personal study or in the chapters you read from the *Unglued* book?
- How did the last session impact your daily life or your relationship with God?
- What questions would you like to ask the other members of your group?

Video: *Four Kinds of Unglued* (20 MINUTES)

Play the video segment for Session 3. As you watch, use the outline (pages 73–76) to follow along or to take notes on anything that stands out to you.

Notes

There is only one thing a carousel does well—go around and around and around.

We have a choice: the easy reaction or the good reaction.

Like the carousel, we can ride the merry-go-round of life, choosing the easy reactions, repeating the same mistakes, and never really making any forward progress.

Setting a pattern of choosing easy over good is a slippery slope. Easy isn't the new good.

"He has showed you, O man, what is good. And what does the LORD require of you? To act justly and to love mercy and to walk humbly with your God" (Micah 6:8 NIV 1984).

Exploding means pushing emotions outward.

Stuffing means pushing emotions inward.

Four categories of unglued reactions:

1. Exploders who shame themselves

> When I take the easy route, I let the situation dictate my reaction. When I am determined to pursue the good, I rise up and unexpectedly give grace. I give grace because I so desperately need grace.

2. Exploders who blame others

> When I take the easy route, I blame others for pushing me into this undesirable place emotionally. When I am determined to pursue the good, I remember I'm not a slave to my feelings.

3. Stuffers who build barriers

> When I take the easy route, I stuff down the aggravation and hurt and build a barrier to hide behind. When I am determined to pursue the good, I establish boundaries that communicate what I really want.

4. Stuffers who collect retaliation rocks

> When I take the easy route, I smile and swallow and form these bitter rocks and wait for the right moment to pull them out and retaliate with proof. When I am determined to pursue the good, I remember that true peacekeeping is about properly processing my emotions before they get stuffed.

Soul integrity is honesty that's godly.

Imperfect progress moves us forward. It keeps us from circling the same old reactions, just like circling around on that carousel.

"You are the salt of the earth. But if the salt loses its saltiness, how can it be made salty again? It is no longer good for anything, except to be thrown out and trampled by men. You are the light of the world. A city on a hill cannot be hidden" (Matthew 5:13 – 14 NIV 1984).

Group Discussion

Video Debrief (5 MINUTES)

If your group meets for two hours, allow 10 minutes for this discussion.

1. What part of the video teaching had the most impact on you?

Easy vs. Good (10 MINUTES)

If your group meets for two hours, allow 25 minutes for this discussion.

2. On the DVD, Lysa likened choosing the easy path—repeating mistakes and bad habits—to a carousel that goes around and around but never makes forward progress. When you consider your imperfect progress over the last couple of weeks, place a checkmark next to the carnival ride

or game that comes closest to describing your experience of progress. Share the reasons for your response.

☐ Bumper cars	☐ Tea cups	☐ Bounce house
☐ Big slide	☐ Water slide	☐ Ball pit
☐ Drop tower	☐ Zip line	☐ Skeeball
☐ Ferris wheel	☐ Obstacle course	☐ Air hockey
☐ Roller coaster	☐ Mechanical bull	☐ Other:

3. Making forward progress requires pursuing the *good* over the *easy*. In the book of Micah, the Bible provides a compelling statement about how God defines good (Micah 6:8). But it's important to first understand the context that precedes this statement. God has a case against Israel (Micah 6:1 – 5). Despite God's faithfulness, His people have hated good and loved evil (Micah 3:2). In response to God's charges against them, the people scramble to make amends for their failures:

> What can we bring to the LORD? What kind of offerings should we give him? Should we bow before God with offerings of yearling calves? Should we offer him thousands of rams and ten thousand rivers of olive oil? Should we sacrifice our firstborn children to pay for our sins? (Micah 6:6 – 7 NLT)

It's at this point that the prophet Micah steps in and tells the Israelites that they've completely missed the point about what is good and what God requires of them.

Go around the group and have a different person read aloud each of the three versions of Micah 6:8 that follow. As the passages are read, underline any words or phrases that stand out to you. You may wish to read through the list twice to give everyone time to listen and respond.

> He has shown you, O mortal, what is good. And what does the LORD require of you? To act justly and to love mercy and to walk humbly with your God. (NIV)

> The LORD God has told us what is right and what he demands: "See that justice is done, let mercy be your first concern, and humbly obey your God." (CEV)

> But he's already made it plain how to live, what to do, what God is looking for in men and women. It's quite simple: Do what is fair and just to your neighbor, be compassionate and loyal in your love, and don't take yourself too seriously—take God seriously. (MSG)

- How might the Israelites' initial response represent a choice of easy (Micah 6:6–7) over good (Micah 6:8)? What would their response have required — and not required — of them?

- God's definition of what is good stipulates two requirements for our human relationships (*act justly, love mercy*) and one overarching requirement for our relationship with God (*walk humbly*). Using the three versions of Micah 6:8 as a reference, how would you describe what it might mean to choose the good over the easy in connection with raw emotions? Consider all three requirements: act justly, love mercy, walk humbly.

Four Unglued Reactions (8 MINUTES)

If your group meets for two hours, allow 20 minutes for this discussion.

4. Lysa described four unglued reactions:

> *Exploders who shame themselves*
> *Exploders who blame others*
> *Stuffers who build barriers*
> *Stuffers who collect retaliation rocks*

- If you were to ask the people who know you best to describe your tendency, which of the four reactions would they say is most characteristic of you? What evidence might they cite in support of their choice?

- In what ways does this characteristic reaction represent a choice of easy over good for you?

Optional Individual Activity and Group Discussion:
Understanding Unglued Reactions (20 MINUTES)

If your group meets for two hours, include this activity as part of your meeting. Allow 20 minutes total—5 minutes for the individual activity and 15 minutes for the group discussion.

Individual Activity (5 MINUTES)

Complete this activity on your own.

1. Take a moment to identify two recent unglued experiences—one in which you were an exploder who pushed emotions outward, and one in which you were a stuffer who pushed emotions inward. You may find it helpful to refer to the charts from the personal study on pages 63–64, or to review any field notes you wrote on pages 37–39 and 70–72.

2. Briefly describe your behavior for each reaction (just one or two sentences). Also note whether you were an exploder who shamed yourself or blamed others, or a stuffer who built barriers or collected retaliation rocks.

> My experience of being an exploder . . .

> My experience of being a stuffer . . .

Group Discussion (15 MINUTES)

1. If you feel comfortable, briefly describe one of your reactions: how you shamed or blamed after an exploder experience; or how you built barriers or collected retaliation rocks after a stuffer experience. What was the impact of your reaction—on you and on the other person?

2. Depending on the situation and the people involved, we might shift our unglued reactions.
   - What situations and people tend to elicit an exploder response from you? Which tend to elicit a stuffer response?
   - How do you account for the shift in your responses?

3. How would you assess your unglued tendency as a group? When you are together, would you say you tend to be a group of exploders or a group of stuffers? What implications might this tendency have for you as a participant in the group, and for the group as a whole?

Soul Integrity (10 MINUTES)

If your group meets for two hours, allow 20 minutes for this discussion.

5. In processing unglued reactions, our goal is soul integrity. Soul integrity is honesty that's godly. It means refusing to choose the easy over the good.

   Exploders choose the easy over the good when they embrace a semblance of honesty but refuse to be reined in by godliness. Stuffers choose the easy over the good when they embrace a semblance of godliness (peacemaking) but refuse to be reined in by honesty.

   • Using this framework, how would you characterize the Israelites' initial response to God (Micah 6:6 – 7)? Did they embrace a semblance of honesty but refuse to be reined in by godliness? Or did they embrace a semblance of godliness but refuse to be reined in by honesty?

   • Do you think something similar could be true for you? In other words, how might your unglued tendency impact the way you relate to God?

   • A soul with integrity is whole and undivided. How would you describe your desire for soul integrity? What impact do you hope this practice of honesty that's godly will have on you?

6. Briefly reflect on what you've learned and experienced together in *Unglued* so far.

   • Since the first session, how have you experienced God's grace in connection with your raw emotions?

- What shifts have you noticed in yourself in terms of how you relate to the group? For example, do you feel more or less guarded, understood, challenged, encouraged, connected, etc.?

- What adjustments, if any, would you like the other group members to make on their Session 1 chart (pages 18 – 19) to help them be better companions for you?

Individual Activity: *What I Want to Remember* (2 MINUTES)

Complete this activity on your own.

1. Briefly review the outline and any notes you took.
2. In the space below, write down the most significant thing you gained in this session — from the teaching, activities, or discussions.

   What I want to remember from this session . . .

Closing Prayer

Close your time together with prayer.

Between Now and the Next Session

In the upcoming personal studies, you'll have an opportunity to continue taking field notes on your unglued experiences. The focus this week is on gaining God's perspective on our struggles, developing holy restraint, and pursuing soul integrity. In the last study of the week, you'll also have a chance to celebrate your imperfect progress so far. So be on the lookout for every sign of grace!

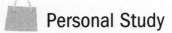

Personal Study

● DAY 1: **Study and Reflect**

> Raw emotions will come. And when they do, they won't sit quietly still awaiting further instructions.
>
> *Unglued*, page 61

1. Raw emotions can be like bossy generals, always barking out orders. And when raw emotions lock eyes with the person on the other side of a conflict, the bossy general within often has just one thought: *It's you against me.*

   Identify a current or recent conflict. On the diagram that follows, imagine that the person with whom you have a conflict is on the left and you are on the right. Below the diagram, briefly describe how you experience this person as an enemy. For example, how is this person hostile to you or trying to do damage to you? How do you understand the balance of power between you? What is at stake if you win or lose?

   You   Against   Me

> In God's economy, people don't stand on opposing sides of the conflict scale. People stand on one side and Satan stands on the other. When we dump hurt into one another's lives, we aren't leveling the conflict scale. We are just weighing down the people side of the scale and elevating the Satan side of the scale.... The secret to healthy conflict resolution isn't taking a you-against-me stance, but realizing it's all of us against Satan — he's the real enemy.
>
> *Unglued*, pages 64 – 65

2. In processing unglued reactions, our goal is soul integrity—honesty that's godly. Holding onto soul integrity requires first stepping back from the fray so we can see our struggle from God's point of view. Here is how the apostle Paul describes God's perspective on our hardships:

> For our struggle is not against flesh and blood, but against the rulers, against the authorities, against the powers of this dark world and against the spiritual forces of evil in the heavenly realms. (Ephesians 6:12)

Now imagine that you and the person you identified in question 1 are together as "us" on the left side of the diagram below. How does identifying the real enemy shift your perspective on the conflict? For example, how is the real enemy hostile to or trying to do damage to "us"? How do you understand the balance of power between "us" and the real enemy? What is at stake if "us" wins or loses?

Us   Against   The Real Enemy

> A moment of conflict handled the right way is hands-down one of the grandest opportunities we have to shame Satan back to hell. A Jesus girl who rises up and unexpectedly gives grace when she surely could have done otherwise, reveals the power and the mystery of Christ at work—in her life and in the world.
>
> *Unglued*, page 65

3. One way to give grace in the midst of conflict is to choose a *reply* over a *reaction*. A reply is simply a response, like a gentle answer to a question. But a reaction is much more than a response—it's oppositional energy in motion. The wise writer of Proverbs describes the vital difference between the two:

> A gentle answer deflects anger, but harsh words make tempers flare (Proverbs 15:1 NLT).

We might adapt this verse to read: *A gentle reply deflects anger, but harsh reactions lead straight to the great unglued!*

What *reactions* took place in the conflict you identified for questions 1 and 2? Write down two or three of your statements or behaviors that could be characterized as oppositional energy in motion.

For each reaction you wrote down, now write an *alternative* reply. What might you have said or done to deflect rather than amplify tensions?

It may seem that choosing a gentle reply is a sign of weakness. In fact, it is a rare and godly strength — one that Jesus used to describe Himself: "I am gentle and humble in heart" (Matthew 11:29). And the apostle Paul and other New Testament writers repeatedly name gentleness as a defining characteristic of Jesus' followers:

Always be humble and gentle. Be patient with each other, making allowance for each other's faults because of your love. (Ephesians 4:2 NLT)

Make a clean break with all cutting, backbiting, profane talk. Be gentle with one another, sensitive. (Ephesians 4:31 MSG)

Let your gentleness be evident to all. The Lord is near. (Philippians 4:5)

But the wisdom from above is first of all pure. It is also peace loving, gentle at all times, and willing to yield to others. (James 3:17 NLT)

You should clothe yourselves instead with the beauty that comes from within, the unfading beauty of a gentle and quiet spirit, which is so precious to God. (1 Peter 3:4 NLT)

Based on these verses, how would you describe what it means to be gentle? Use three to five words or phrases to complete the sentence:

To be gentle is to be ...

How have you recently experienced this kind of gentleness in your relationship with God?

Based on your experience of God's gentleness, how would you describe the power or strength that is the foundation of gentleness?

Guided Prayer

God, thank You for giving me Your perspective on my relational struggles. It's not always easy in the midst of conflict, but it helps me to remember who the real enemy is.

Today, I ask for Your grace in my relationship with ... Give me the courage and strength I need to be gentle. I think You may be inviting me to be gentle by ... This is hard for me because ...

God, Your gentleness has been a saving grace to me more times than I can count. Help me today to practice this same gentleness with the people You have put in my life. Amen.

The Week Ahead

This week, you'll use the charts on pages 101 – 103 to continue taking field notes as you did for Sessions 1 and 2, but now with one additional question: *Was my reaction characterized by exploding or stuffing?*

Allow a few minutes of your reading and study time each day to briefly document your experiences. Remember that the purpose of writing things down is not to beat yourself up, but to raise awareness and to continue measuring imperfect progress.

● DAY 2: **Read and Learn**

Use the charts on pages 101 – 103 to briefly document any observations about your emotions and reactions over the last twenty-four hours (see page 25 for guidance and examples).

Read chapter 5 of the *Unglued* book. Use the space below to note any insights or questions you want to bring to the next group session.

● DAY 3: **Study and Reflect**

Use the charts on pages 101 – 103 to briefly document any observations about your emotions and reactions over the last twenty-four hours (see page 25 for guidance and examples).

> Holy restraint is the internal experience of living with Christ and really applying His truths to my life. It's deciding I'm not just going to *ingest* His truths by taking them in and feeling good about them for a few minutes. I'm going to *digest* His truths by making them part of who I am and how I live.... That's what it means to have an internal experience with Him. Only then will we develop holy restraint. This holy restraint will hold us back when we want to aggressively charge ahead. It will help us hold our tongue when we want to instantly cut loose with the yelling. It will help us pause before blasting someone in an emotional tirade.
>
> *Unglued*, pages 75 – 76

1. When a relationship is stressful, it's easy to pray that holy restraint would somehow miraculously take hold of the other person. It's much harder to be still in God's presence, digest His truths, and be willing to pray, *Dear God, please let holy restraint take hold of me.*

     How would you describe the degree to which you are able to experience holy restraint in your stressful relationships right now?

   What connections do you make between your ability to experience holy restraint and the time you spend alone with God?

2. Read "Finding the Quiet" on pages 89–90. Then use the five benefits Lysa describes as a framework for reflecting on a current conflict or stressful relationship.

   The person I'm struggling with right now:

   In the quiet, we feel safe enough to humble ourselves. Consider any weaknesses, blind spots, or mistakes you may have brought to the relationship. In what ways have you intentionally or unintentionally contributed to the conflict?

In the quiet, God lifts us up to a more rational place. To what degree might you have lost perspective on this relationship — perhaps magnifying the conflict or spinning out worst-case scenarios that make it difficult for you to hope for resolution?

In the quiet, anxiety gives way to progress. What fears and anxieties do you have about this relationship?

In the quiet, we acknowledge that our real enemy isn't the other person. How might the real enemy be at work in this conflict? Where are you especially aware of a need for self-control to help you resist and stand firm?

In the quiet, we can rest assured that God will use this conflict for good — no matter how it turns out. What good do you hope God might be working in you through this conflict?

Finding the Quiet

We're dealing with emotions and relationships ... both of which are like nailing Jell-O to the wall. It's a complicated, messy, and unpredictable process, for sure. Sometimes a girl can get worn out, wonder if she's ever going to stop exploding, and feel like giving up. But before I give up, I've learned to hush up. This often means hitting some sort of pause button on whatever situation is making me feel like exploding. Ideally, this would mean getting away by myself in the quiet of my home. But sometimes it means excusing myself to the restroom. Bathroom stalls can make great prayer closets (smiles). The point is that the only way I can see what God is doing and attend to what He reveals is to get quiet with Him.

Of course, it's hard to be quiet when I'm in a potentially exploding frame of mind. But [here are] five beautiful things I've discovered in the quiet, five things that are balm for the raw edges of a soul on the precipice of exploding.

1. In the quiet, we feel safe enough to humble ourselves. The last thing I want to do in the heat of an emotional mess is to be humble. I want to be loud, proud, and prove my point. But I've learned the hard way that I have to step out of the battle and humbly ask God to speak truth to my heart in order for things to start making sense. Never have I had a relationship issue in which I didn't contribute at least something to the problem. Usually, I can only see this something in the quiet. The quiet is what enables us to "humble [ourselves], therefore, under God's mighty hand" (1 Peter 5:6).

2. In the quiet, God lifts us up to a more rational place. When we are in the heat of a tangled mess, crazy emotions drag us down into a pit of hopelessness. The only way out of the pit is to make the choice to stop digging deeper and turn to God for a solution, so "that [God] may lift you up in due time" (1 Peter 5:6).

3. In the quiet, anxiety gives way to progress. We can pour out our anxious hearts to Jesus who loves us right where we are, just as we are. Because His love comes without unfair human judgment, we soften and feel safe enough to humbly admit we need

Him to work on us. Trying to fix another person only adds to my anxiety. Letting Jesus work on me is where real progress happens. I claim the promise that says, "Cast all your anxiety on him because he cares for you" (1 Peter 5:7).

4. In the quiet, we acknowledge that our real enemy isn't the other person. This person with whom we're in conflict may seem like the enemy and might even look like the enemy. But the truth is, that person isn't the real culprit. The real culprit is Satan, who is exerting influence on both me and on the person offending me. I don't always realize this in the heat of the moment, but in the quiet, I can remind myself of the truth and choose a strategy for responding with self-control. That's the wisdom of Scripture, which says, "Be self-controlled and alert. Your enemy the devil prowls around like a roaring lion looking for someone to devour. Resist him, standing firm in the faith" (1 Peter 5:8 – 9 NIV 1984).

5. In the quiet, we can rest assured God will use this conflict for good — no matter how it turns out. If I make the effort to handle this conflict well, I can be freed from the pressure to make everything turn out rosy. Sometimes relationships grow stronger through conflict; other times relationships end. Because I can't control the other person, I must focus on the good God is working out in me through this situation and leave the outcome with Him. God's Word promises that "the God of all grace, who called you to his eternal glory in Christ, after you have suffered a little while, will himself restore you and make you strong, firm, and steadfast" (1 Peter 5:10 – 11).

Unglued, pages 76 – 78

3. Take a few moments to spend time with God in quiet right now, inviting Him to speak to you about the relationship you're struggling with.

   • After reading through the remaining bullet points, set aside your study materials and settle into a comfortable place.

   • To avoid being distracted about time, you may wish to set a timer for 5 – 10 minutes or however much time you are able to spend in silence.

   • Begin by inviting God to be with you. You might pray, "Come, Holy Spirit," "Jesus, be present with me," or "Speak, Lord, Your servant listens." If your mind is full of distracting thoughts that make it difficult to be still, briefly name those concerns and ask God to hold them for you.

   • Invite God to speak to you about your relationship. Then rest quietly in silence, trusting that you are in the presence of a loving God who knows what you need.

   • Close your time by thanking God for His presence with you.

   Resist any temptation to judge your time of silent listening as a "success" or "failure." God is always at work, even when we can't feel it. Whatever the outcome, we can rest in the knowledge that God is always pleased with our desire to spend time with Him in quiet.

Guided Prayer

God, thank You for wanting to spend time with me. I believe You are always at work in my life and always out to do me good.

I know that holy restraint is an expression of Your goodness, and I want to experience more of it in my life. I especially need holy restraint to take hold of me when . . .

Lord, increase my desire to spend time with You in the quiet. Teach me how to be present with You in the same way You are present with me. Amen.

● DAY 4: **Read and Learn**

Use the charts on pages 101 – 103 to briefly document any observations about your emotions and reactions over the last twenty-four hours (see page 25 for guidance and examples).

Read chapter 6 of the *Unglued* book. Use the space below to note any insights or questions you want to bring to the next group session.

● DAY 5: **Study and Reflect**

Use the charts on pages 101 – 103 to briefly document any observations about your emotions and reactions over the last twenty-four hours (see page 25 for guidance and examples).

> Have you ever tried to keep the peace by avoiding confrontation and pretending that everything is fine? I have. I just stuff down the negative emotions. And it hurts. It hurts me. It hurts the other person. And it certainly hurts the relationship, which slowly erodes. What seems like peace on the outside is actually the muffled roar of barrier-building on the inside.
>
> *Unglued*, pages 83 – 84

1. Which reasons typically lead you to avoid confrontation by pretending everything is fine? Check all that apply.

☐ I don't feel safe enough to confront this person.

☐ I don't have the energy or the time to get into a conflict.

☐ I don't know how to address it.

☐ I don't want to seem hypersensitive.

☐ I don't want to be rejected.

☐ I don't want to lose control.

☐ I don't want to make things worse, so I convince myself I can just let it go.

☐ I don't want to be perceived as ungodly.

☐ Other:

Of the reasons you checked, which would you say was primary in your most recent experience of stuffing? (You may wish to refer to your field notes on pages 37–39, 70–72.) Circle the reason on the list that stands out most to you.

Briefly reflect on the reason behind this reason by asking the "why" question. For example: *Why is it important to me to know how to address it? Why is it important to me to stay in control? Why is it important to me to be perceived as godly?* Use the sentence starter below to write down your question.

As much as possible, keep your response to the question focused on yourself rather than the other person. For example, even if it is the other person's aggressive behavior that makes you feel unsafe, cultivate curiosity about your own emotions and behaviors when you feel unsafe rather than focusing on the other person's behavior.

Question: *Why is it important to me to …*

Imagine that you are interviewing yourself about the response you just wrote down. What might you be curious about? Write down one or two additional questions you might ask yourself and then write your responses.

Question 1:

Question 2:

In what ways, if any, do your responses to the *why* question and to your own question(s) help you to understand more about yourself or your relationships?

> Barriers shut down communication. When you determine other people aren't safe, you label them with words such as *demanding*, *irresponsible*, *volatile*, *selfish*, and *defensive*. No matter what they do or don't do, this barrier label is the filter through which you process everything about them. Mentally, you just stick it across a person's name in your brain. The problem is: They don't know it's there. So every interaction confuses them. They know something is wrong but have no clue what it is. Eventually, this relationship will shrivel up and die because it's been deprived of open communication, the life-giving oxygen that fuels good relationships.
>
> *Unglued*, page 84

2. Use the left column on the chart that follows (page 95) to identify two or three people with whom you have chosen to avoid confrontation by stuffing your emotions. Use the remaining columns to write down three to five mental labels you have for each person and how these labels and your stuffing overall has impacted the relationship.

> I can't ignore the obvious issues and hope things will somehow miraculously get better on their own. *I* have to get better. I have to take the necessary steps to keep my soul integrity intact. I have to pursue being the person God wants me to be regardless of how other people react.
>
> *Unglued*, page 90

PEOPLE WITH WHOM I HAVE AVOIDED CONFRONTATION	MENTAL LABELS I HAVE ATTACHED TO THIS PERSON	THE IMPACT MY STUFFING HAS HAD ON OUR RELATIONSHIP

3. Soul integrity is honesty that's godly. As you reflect on your chart and the impact stuffing emotions has had on your relationships, what cracks are you aware of in your soul integrity?

The apostle Paul offers these guidelines for keeping relational soul integrity intact:

> Never pay back evil with more evil. Do things in such a way that everyone can see you are honorable. Do all that you can to live in peace with everyone. (Romans 12:17 – 18 NLT)

Using the relationships you wrote on your chart as a reference, how might these guidelines help you take the necessary steps to begin reclaiming your soul integrity?

I can refuse to pay back evil with more evil by . . .

I can choose to be honorable by . . .

Doing all that I can to live in peace might include . . .

Guided Prayer

God, thank You for making it possible for me to be at peace with You.

I want to experience that same peace in my relationships, but I have some-times sacrificed my soul integrity to get it. This has caused pain for me and for people I care about. I especially need Your help with...

Lord, be my Prince of Peace. I want to honor You in all of my relationships. Give me the strength I need today to pursue honesty that's godly. Amen.

● DAY 6: Gentle Noticing

The personal studies this week provided an opportunity for you to continue taking field notes on your raw emotions and reactions. If you weren't able to make notes during the week, do so now. Use the charts on pages 101 – 103 to describe two or three raw emotions or reactions you experienced this week. For guidance and examples, see page 25.

1. Briefly review two things: (1) what you wrote on your charts this week (pages 101 – 103), and (2) what you wrote in response to question 1 from last week's Day 6 study (pages 66 – 68). What similarities or differences do you notice between last week and this week in the following areas?

   The frequency of my raw emotions/reactions this week compared to last week ...

The people who prompt my raw emotions/reactions this week compared to last week . . .

My physical and emotional state before the events of this week compared to last week . . .

What happened that prompted my raw emotions/reactions this week compared to last week . . .

How I reacted this week compared to last week . . .

How my reactions were characterized by exploding or stuffing this week compared to last week ...

The words and phrases I used to label myself afterward ...

Additional observations about this week compared to last week ...

2. How did you experience God at work in you this week? For example: in experiences of grace, gentle chiseling, or imperfect progress?

3. This session marks the halfway point in the *Unglued* curriculum. Congratulations for persevering in your imperfect progress! In any journey, celebrating progress at the halfway point is a great way to find new energy and focus for the second half. As you think back over your

experiences, studies, and field notes from the first half of this journey, what changes or progress can you celebrate?

Guided Prayer

God, thank You for Your endless supply of grace for me. Your gentle chiseling gives me hope that I really can make progress.

Today, I ask You for courage to stay on this journey and to continue taking next steps. Some of the next steps I sense You may be inviting me to take are ... I need Your help to follow through because ...

I entrust myself and my imperfect progress to You. Please give me the desire and the power to do what pleases You each day. And keep chiseling me! Amen.

PERSON	FIELD NOTES ON MY RAW REACTIONS
	1. What was my physical and emotional state before the event?
	2. What happened that prompted my raw reaction?
	3. How did I react?
	4. Was my reaction characterized by exploding or stuffing? Write "E" in the margin for exploding or "S" in the margin for stuffing.
	5. What words or phrases did I use to mentally label myself afterward?

PERSON	FIELD NOTES ON MY RAW REACTIONS
	1. What was my physical and emotional state before the event?
	2. What happened that prompted my raw reaction?
	3. How did I react?
	4. Was my reaction characterized by exploding or stuffing? Write "E" in the margin for exploding or "S" in the margin for stuffing.
	5. What words or phrases did I use to mentally label myself afterward?

PERSON	FIELD NOTES ON MY RAW REACTIONS
	1. What was my physical and emotional state before the event?
	2. What happened that prompted my raw reaction?
	3. How did I react?
	4. Was my reaction characterized by exploding or stuffing? Write "E" in the margin for exploding or "S" in the margin for stuffing.
	5. What words or phrases did I use to mentally label myself afterward?

A Procedure Manual
for the Unglued

Group Discussion: *Checking In* (5 MINUTES)

If your group meets for two hours, allow 10 minutes for this discussion.

Welcome to Session 4 of *Unglued*. A key part of getting to know God better is sharing your journey with others. Before watching the video, briefly check in with each other about your experiences since the last session. For example:

- What insights did you discover in the personal study or in the chapters you read from the *Unglued* book?
- How did the last session impact your daily life or your relationship with God?
- What questions would you like to ask the other members of your group?

Video: *A Procedure Manual for the Unglued* (16 MINUTES)

Play the video segment for Session 4. As you watch, use the outline (pages 105–106) to follow along or to take notes on anything that stands out to you.

Notes

The sculpting process requires a plan to follow.

When we feel unglued, we need a procedure manual to follow.

Five principles (based on King Jehoshaphat's story in 2 Chronicles 20)

1. Remember who you are.

2. Redirect your focus to Jesus.

3. Recognize God's job isn't your job.

4. Recite praises and thanks to God.

5. Realize that reactions determine reach.

Group Discussion

Video Debrief (5 MINUTES)

If your group meets for two hours, allow 10 minutes for this discussion.

1. What part of the video teaching had the most impact on you?

A Plan for the Process (7 MINUTES)

If your group meets for two hours, allow 15 minutes for this discussion.

2. Antonio, the sculptor Lysa met, told her about the joys of watching a work of art emerge from a raw piece of marble during the sculpting process.

   • Briefly describe a recent experience you had of watching something good emerge from raw material. It might be as simple as cooking a recipe from scratch or as complex as creating a presentation for work or teaching a child to ride a bike. How would you describe the process of going from raw material to the something good that resulted? Was it short and sweet? Long and complicated? What did you enjoy most and least about the process itself?

   • How important was it to follow a clear process or plan—did it matter a little or a lot? To what degree might the outcome have changed if you hadn't followed any process or plan?

3. What was your initial reaction to the idea of having a plan or a procedure manual to manage your unglued reactions? What similarities and differences do you see between the experience you described in question 2 and your own process of being chiseled into something new?

Begin with the End in Mind (15 MINUTES)

If your group meets for two hours, allow 30 minutes for this discussion.

4. The story of King Jehoshaphat begins in crazy and ends in calm. His story is instructive because following a God-honoring process that takes us from crazy to calm is a big part of what the *Unglued* journey is all about.

   Using the chart that follows, read aloud the four versions of the text that describe the beginning and end of King Jehoshaphat's story. Keeping in mind how this story might provide a parallel for your own unglued experiences, underline any words or phrases that stand out to you.

HOW THE STORY BEGINS (2 CHRONICLES 20:3)	HOW THE STORY ENDS (2 CHRONICLES 20:30)
Alarmed, Jehoshaphat resolved to inquire of the LORD. (NIV)	And the kingdom of Jehoshaphat was at peace, for his God had given him rest on every side. (NIV)
Jehoshaphat was terrified by this news and begged the LORD for guidance. (NLT)	So Jehoshaphat's kingdom was at peace, for his God had given him rest on every side. (NLT)
Shaken, Jehoshaphat prayed. (MSG)	As long as Jehoshaphat reigned, peace reigned. (MSG)
Jehoshaphat was afraid, so he asked the LORD what to do. (CEV)	The LORD let Jehoshaphat's kingdom be at peace. (CEV)

- What connections do you make between the king's emotional state at the beginning of the story and your own starting point in addressing raw emotions? (If you completed the Session 1 personal studies, you may wish to refer back to your starting point statement on page 35 or to your field notes on pages 37–39.)

- Beginning with the end in mind requires faith — we identify what we want but don't yet have. Then we choose our first steps strategically for their ability to move us closer to what we want. How do you recognize the seeds of this principle at work at the beginning of Jehoshaphat's story?

- The verses describing the end of Jehoshaphat's story emphasize rest and peace. Briefly describe the "end" you hope for (what you want but don't yet have) in connection with your raw emotions and reactions. (If you completed the Session 1 personal studies, you may wish to refer back to your goal statement on page 36.) To what degree has keeping the end in mind influenced your first steps or motivated you to keep pursuing imperfect progress?

Jehoshaphat's Procedure Manual (11 MINUTES)

If your group meets for two hours, allow 20 minutes for this discussion.

5. Between the panic that begins Jehoshaphat's story and the peace that ends it, the king's actions provide a compelling framework for bringing our own unglued reactions to a peaceful end:

1. Remember who you are. (2 Chronicles 20:2–4)
2. Redirect your focus to Jesus. (2 Chronicles 20:12b–13)
3. Recognize God's job isn't your job. (2 Chronicles 20:14–17)
4. Recite praises and thanks to God. (2 Chronicles 20:18–22)
5. Realize that reactions determine reach. (2 Chronicles 20:23–30)

As a group, choose two of these steps to discuss in greater depth. (If time permits, it's definitely worthwhile to discuss all five steps!) Use the following questions to discuss each step.

• Read aloud the corresponding text in your Bible for one of the steps you chose.

• How do you understand the connection between this step, the text, and what it means to take this step in response to your own raw emotions?

• What challenges might make it difficult for you to follow through on this step?

• In what ways, if any, does this step and/or Jehoshaphat's story encourage you or give you hope for your own struggles?

Optional Group Discussion: *Get the Whole Story* (23 MINUTES)

If your group meets for two hours, include this discussion as part of your meeting.

1. Using your Bibles and taking a few verses at a time, go around the group and read Jehoshaphat's story aloud (2 Chronicles 20:1–30).

2. What details in the story stand out most to you? Why?

3. The story includes a detailed account of Jehoshaphat's prayer (2 Chronicles 20:6–20).

   • What insights does the king's prayer provide about asking God for help? For example: How does the king address God? How does he make his case and describe what is at stake? What else do you notice about the prayer?

   • How does the king's prayer help you understand what it might mean for you to ask God for help with your raw emotions and reactions?

4. The king never acts alone. He rallies everyone in his kingdom to fast, pray, wait on the Lord, and prepare themselves for battle.

   • To what degree would you say you are rallying help in your efforts to make progress with raw emotions and reactions — a little, a lot, or somewhere between? How has this impacted your progress?

   • What concerns you or intrigues you about inviting other people to be more involved in helping you?

6. Briefly touch base with each other about what you're learning and how you're doing in the group. Use one of the sentence starters below, or your own statement, to help the group learn more about the best way to be a good companion to you.

I want to give you permission to challenge me more about . . .

An area where I really need your help or sensitivity is . . .

It always helps me to feel more connected to the group when . . .

Something I've learned about myself because of this group is . . .

Individual Activity: *What I Want to Remember* (2 MINUTES)

Complete this activity on your own.

1. Briefly review the outline and any notes you took.
2. In the space below, write down the most significant thing you gained in this session—from the teaching, activities, or discussions.

   What I want to remember from this session . . .

Closing Prayer

Close your time together with prayer.

Personal Study

● DAY 1: **Study and Reflect**

Use the charts on pages 131 – 133 to briefly document any observations about your emotions and reactions over the last twenty-four hours (see page 25 for guidance and examples).

> Instead of avoiding the reality that I come unglued, I'm tackling it head-on. I want to give myself every fighting chance to make wise choices in the midst of raw emotions. And having a predetermined plan is a good thing to create and implement. Care to join me? Not that your plan will look the same as mine. Feel free to take this idea and make it your own. The best kind of plan for you is the one you'll follow.
>
> *Unglued*, page 117

In the Day 1 and Day 3 personal studies this week, you'll have a chance to do more in-depth study on the five steps of King Jehoshaphat's story (from the group session) in order to develop your own predetermined plan for making wise choices in the midst of raw emotions. The five steps are:

1. Remember who you are.
2. Redirect your focus to Jesus.
3. Recognize God's job isn't your job.
4. Recite praises and thanks to God.
5. Realize that reactions determine reach.

You'll focus on steps 1 – 3 today and steps 4 – 5 in the Day 3 study. On Day 3, you'll also review all five steps to adjust and finalize them, and then summarize your plan in a short version to make it easy to remember.

1. In your Bible, read the first half of King Jehoshaphat's story in 2 Chronicles 20:1 – 17.

Step 1: Remember Who You Are

Alarmed, Jehoshaphat *resolved*. The king had *resolved* to inquire of the Lord. This is how I want to be. When I feel alarmed, I want to simultaneously be resolved. *Alarmed*, Lysa *resolved*. And here's what I want to be resolved to do — to remember who I am. . . .

I am not an unglued woman who is a slave to her circumstances, her hormones, or to other people's attitudes. Those things might affect me, but they don't rule me. I am a child of God, holy and dearly loved, whom God has set apart for a mighty plan.

Unglued, pages 108, 109

2. To be *unresolved* is to be hesitant, wavering, aimless. To be *resolved* is to be determined, tenacious, and purposeful. As you move into the second half of *Unglued*, how would you assess your overall level of resolve to continue working on your raw emotions and reactions? Place an ✗ on the continuum to indicate your response.

●————————————————————————————————————●
Unresolved   Resolved

One way to strengthen overall resolve is to shift your focus from a big task to a small step. In response to alarm about an impending enemy attack, King Jehoshaphat didn't resolve to defeat the enemy (big task), but to inquire of the Lord (small step). In response to unglued emotions, Lysa resolved to make her small step remembering who she is — a child of God — before tackling the big task of how to respond.

What thoughts or emotions typically characterize your very first experience in a conflict or stressful situation? Focus on that brief moment before you say or do anything in response. For example: *I think things like, "I have to get out of here," "I hate you," or "You make me crazy." I lock into command-and-control mode. I go blank. I get ready to fight. I try not to cry. I go from zero to sixty on the anger meter.* Write down three to five thoughts or emotions that characterize your first experience in conflict or stressful situations.

What small step might help you to redirect the thoughts and emotions you just identified? You could follow Jehoshaphat's or Lysa's example, or identify your own small step. For example: *I will remind myself that God is here with me. This person is not my real enemy. God is in control. God is my shield. The Lord is my strength.* Write a potential small step for each of the thoughts and emotions you identified in the previous question. (For now, you are only collecting your thoughts and developing ideas for your plan. You'll come back to adjust and finalize each step of your plan when you complete the Day 3 study.)

Step 2: Redirect Your Focus to Jesus

I love the honest admission by King Jehoshaphat and his people. They didn't know what to do, but they knew *who* to turn to. Their attention was fixed on the Lord.

Unglued, page 109

3. When we feel stressed or threatened, simply praying the name of Jesus into the situation surrounds us with protection (Proverbs 18:10). As part of developing a predetermined plan, it can also be helpful to have a predetermined prayer that makes it easy to invite Jesus into our situation.

    Briefly review the two charts that follow. On each chart, place a check next to the two or three statements or titles that stand out most to you.

✓	TEN "I AM" STATEMENTS MADE BY JESUS
	I am gentle and humble in heart. (Matthew 11:29)
	I am with you always. (Matthew 28:20)
	I am among you as one who serves. (Luke 22:27)
	I am the bread of life. (John 6:35)
	I am the light of the world. (John 8:12)
	I am the gate for the sheep. (John 10:7)
	I am the good shepherd. (John 10:14)
	I am the resurrection and the life. (John 11:25)
	I am the way and the truth and the life. (John 14:6)
	I am the vine. (John 15:5)

✓	TEN TITLES FOR JESUS
	Immanuel (Isaiah 7:14)
	Wonderful Counselor (Isaiah 9:6)
	Mighty God (Isaiah 9:6)
	Everlasting Father (Isaiah 9:6)
	Prince of Peace (Isaiah 9:6)
	Lamb of God (John 1:29)
	Rabbi/Teacher (John 1:38)
	Holy and Righteous One (Acts 3:14)
	King of kings and Lord of lords (1 Timothy 6:15)
	Bright Morning Star (Revelation 22:16)

Of the statements and titles you checked, which have the strongest connection to something you need when you are in a conflict or stressful situation? On each chart, circle one of the items you checked.

Use the "I am" statement and title you circled as the basis for two, one-sentence prayers. For example: *Jesus, help me to be humble and gentle* or *Jesus, be my Light. Wonderful Counselor, show me what to do* or *Rabbi, teach me Your ways.* Write both prayers below.

Step 3: Recognize God's Job Isn't Your Job

Ultimately, the responsibility for winning this battle we're facing doesn't belong to us. We're not responsible for figuring it all out. *Our job* is simply to be obedient to God in the midst of what we're facing. *God's job* is results. Obedience positions us in the flow of God's power, working with God's ways instead of against God's ways....

I still have to navigate the realities of my situation, but I won't be doing it in my own strength.... I want to participate in His divine nature rather than wallow in my own bad attitude and insecurities. Then I won't have to huff and puff and pout while trying to figure everything out on my own.

Unglued, pages 112, 114

4. Jesus said of Himself, "I do nothing on my own but speak just what the Father has taught me" (John 8:28). It's a simple but powerful statement about what it means to be obedient—to focus on our job so God can do His.

Staying in the flow of God's power in the midst of conflict or stress requires being obedient to what God's Word teaches about how to use words. On the chart that follows (page 117), briefly review the six verses in the left column. Place a checkmark next to the two or three verses that seem most applicable to what you need when you experience raw emotions. For each verse you check, use the right column to identify one way you can be obedient with your words.

	WHAT GOD'S WORD TEACHES ABOUT USING WORDS	WHEN I AM IN THE MIDST OF CONFLICT OR STRESS, I CAN BE OBEDIENT BY . . .
✓	*Example*: Spouting off before listening to the facts is both shameful and foolish. (Proverbs 18:13 NLT)	*Calmly asking at least two or three clarifying questions before responding to the other person.*
	Those who guard their lips preserve their lives, but those who speak rashly will come to ruin. (Proverbs 13:3)	
	A kind answer soothes angry feelings, but harsh words stir them up. (Proverbs 15:1 CEV)	
	Spouting off before listening to the facts is both shameful and foolish. (Proverbs 18:13 NLT)	
	I promise you that on the day of judgment, everyone will have to account for every careless word they have spoken. (Matthew 12:36 CEV)	
	Bless those who persecute you. Don't curse them; pray that God will bless them. (Romans 12:14 NLT)	
	Don't use foul or abusive language. Let everything you say be good and helpful, so that your words will be an encouragement to those who hear them. (Ephesians 4:29 NLT)	

Guided Prayer

God, thank You for showing me how to develop a plan for change — a plan You can use to help me become more like Jesus.

Even as I continue to develop my plan, I offer it to You. I ask for discernment and guidance, especially about . . .

Thank You for giving me hope that it is possible to make wise decisions even when I feel unglued. Amen.

● DAY 2: **Read and Learn**

Use the charts on pages 131 – 133 to briefly document any observations about your emotions and reactions over the last twenty-four hours (see page 25 for guidance and examples).

Read chapter 7 of the *Unglued* book. Use the space below to note any insights or questions you want to bring to the next group session.

● DAY 3: **Study and Reflect**

Use the charts on pages 131 – 133 to briefly document any observations about your emotions and reactions over the last twenty-four hours (see page 25 for guidance and examples).

In today's study, you'll continue the process you started in the Day 1 study of developing your predetermined plan for making wise choices in the midst of raw emotions.

1. In your Bible, read the second half of King Jehoshaphat's story in 2 Chronicles 20:18 – 30.

Step 4: Recite Thanks and Praises to God

I can't authentically praise God for anything that is wrong or evil, but I sure can shift my focus to all that is right and praise Him for that.... Oh, how powerful it is to shift from an attitude to gratitude and to praise our God in the midst of it all. When I do this, my circumstances may not instantly change, but the way I look at those circumstances certainly does. I stop being blind to all that's right and see so many more reasons to praise God. And when my heart is full of praise, my emotions aren't nearly as prone to coming unglued!

Unglued, page 115

2. In Jehoshaphat's story, the people praise God for "the splendor of his holiness," and thank God because "his love endures forever" (2 Chronicles 20:21). Their praise expresses awe for God and who He is; their thanksgiving expresses gratitude for God's love.

List three to five attributes of God that are most meaningful to you. For example: *God's goodness, righteousness, patience; that God is all-knowing, all-powerful, eternally present.*

List three to five things about God's love that inspire the most gratitude in you. For example: *God's love ... completely turned my life around, enabled me to forgive myself, makes it possible for me to have hope, guides me, helps me to know I'm not alone.*

Combine what you wrote about God's attributes and God's love into two or three praise-and-thanks statements. For example: *God, I praise You for Your goodness and thank You for changing me. God, I praise You that You are all-knowing and thank You for guiding me.*

Step 5: Realize Reactions Determine Reach

Why did the fear of God come upon all who heard about Jehoshaphat's victory? Because in the midst of it all, he honored God with his actions and reactions.... And his reactions positively affected everyone around him, not only people in his own kingdom but even those in surrounding countries.

Unglued, page 116

3. Jehoshaphat's reach—his influence and impact—had a ripple effect. Use the diagram on page 121 to imagine the ripple effect you hope might eventually result from making wise decisions in the midst of raw emotions now.

In the center of the oval, write the name of one person who is most often the recipient of your raw reactions.

If raw reactions were no longer a significant factor in this relationship, who else might potentially benefit? Write the names of one or two individuals or groups in the second circle.

Complete the diagram by considering the individuals or groups who might be positively impacted by the people in the second oval. Write their names in the third oval.

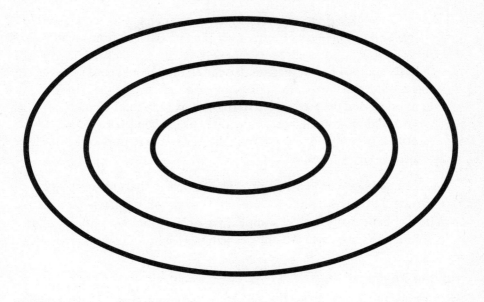

Here's the short version of my predetermined biblical procedure manual all in one place:

1. Alarmed, Lysa resolved to remember who she is.
2. Jesus, Jesus, Jesus.
3. Stay in the flow — my job is obedience, God's job is results.
4. Shift from an attitude to gratitude.
5. Reactions determine my reach.

Unglued, page 117

4. Now that you've worked through all five steps, you're ready to finalize your plan and then summarize it so it's easy to remember. Use the following guidelines to review your work; write your responses to each question in the center column on the chart on page 123. After completing the center column, you'll summarize each step in the right column.

- STEP 1: Which of the small steps you wrote down (page 114) will be most effective in helping you to redirect your thoughts and emotions?
- STEP 2: Which of the two prayers you wrote to invite Jesus into your situation (page 116) do you think will be most helpful to you?
- STEP 3: Which of the ways you identified to be obedient with your words (page 117) will be most effective in helping you to do your job and allow God to do His job?

- STEP 4: Which of the praise-and-thanks statements you wrote down (page 120) will be most effective in helping you to shift from an attitude to gratitude?
- STEP 5: Based on your diagram (page 121), how would you state the reach you hope to have? For example, if the name in the center is a spouse and the second and third ovals include children and grandchildren, you might say something like "I hope to influence everyone from David to the grandkids," or "I want to impact the third generation in our family."

Now go back and use the third column on the chart to summarize each step into a short phrase. You could use the short phrases from Jehoshaphat's story, Lysa's example (page 121), your own phrases, or a combination. Use whatever phrases will be easiest for you to remember.

Guided Prayer

God, thank You for giving me the confidence that comes from following biblical wisdom.

I commit my plan to You, and humbly ask that You give me success (Proverbs 16:3). Help me to remember the steps and to follow through on each one. I especially need Your help with . . .

Lord, I want this plan to be more than just an activity I did in a Bible study. Please use it to change me and to help me become more like You. Amen.

STEPS BASED ON JEHOSHAPHAT'S STORY	STEPS IN MY PLAN	THE SHORT VERSION OF MY PLAN
STEP 1: Remember who you are.	I resolve to …	
STEP 2: Redirect your focus to Jesus.	My Jesus prayer …	
STEP 3: Recognize God's job isn't your job.	How I can do my job (obedience) …	
STEP 4: Recite thanks and praises to God.	My praise and thanks …	
STEP 5: Realize that reactions determine reach.	My reach …	

● DAY 4: **Read and Learn**

Use the charts on pages 131–133 to briefly document any observations about your emotions and reactions over the last twenty-four hours (see page 25 for guidance and examples).

Read chapter 8 of the *Unglued* book. Use the space below to note any insights or questions you want to bring to the next group session.

● DAY 5: **Study and Reflect**

Use the charts on pages 131–133 to briefly document any observations about your emotions and reactions over the last twenty-four hours (see page 25 for guidance and examples).

> The more I rejoice, the more I keep things in perspective. The more I keep things in perspective, the gentler I become.
> That's why I have to intentionally seek out perspective-magnifying opportunities. Things like serving at a soup kitchen, delivering gifts to a family in need, or going on a mission trip. If I want the gentleness inside me to be unleashed, I have to break away from my everyday routine. I have to go where perspective awaits me.
>
> *Unglued*, page 121

1. In his letter to the church at Philippi, the apostle Paul offers a compelling insight on the vital relationship between rejoicing, gentleness, and perspective:

   Rejoice in the Lord always. I will say it again: Rejoice! Let your gentleness be evident to all. The Lord is near. (Philippians 4:4–5)

   For a fresh take on this familiar passage, read it again from *The Message*:

   Celebrate God all day, every day. I mean, revel in him! Make it as clear as you can to all you meet that you're on their side, working with them and not against them. Help them see that the Master is about to arrive. He could show up any minute! (Philippians 4:4–5 MSG)

To revel is to celebrate with intensity and extravagance. How does this perspective help you to understand what it means to revel or rejoice *in the Lord?*

How are you both challenged and encouraged by the idea that gentleness is working *with* someone rather than *against* them?

Keeping things in perspective means considering them in relationship to something larger. How does the truth that "the Lord is near" give you something larger to consider? Specifically, how does it impact your perspective on your relationships, your raw reactions, and your need for gentleness?

2. Read the personal story Lysa shares in "Kid-Placemat Perspective" on page 126. Then respond to the questions that follow.

    Overall, how would you characterize the situations that routinely prompt your raw emotions or reactions? (You may wish to briefly review your field notes on pages 37 – 39, 70 – 72, 101 – 103.) Do these situations tend to be more like slight inconveniences or reasonable things to be alarmed about? Place an ✗ on the continuum to indicate your response.

●━━━━━━━━━━━━━━━━━━━━━━━━━━●

Slight inconveniences   Reasonable things
                                                               to be alarmed about

What is it about these situations that typically makes it difficult for you to see or maintain a larger perspective?

Kid-Placemat Perspective

When my girls were little, we had a love-hate relationship with those paper placemats some fast food restaurants use to entertain kids. I loved that the placemats featured appealing, attention-grabbing pictures and came with complimentary crayons. However, it never failed that someone would color on someone else's placemat and squeals and screams would have all heads in the restaurant turning our way.

Then I would sit there in disbelief that my kids had caused such a fuss over colored-on placemats. Placemats that would soon be covered in ketchup and juice and eventually tossed in the trash. Fleeting things. Insignificant things. I knew my kids wouldn't even remember the placemats tomorrow, let alone a month from now. But for today, the placemats have them coming all unglued.

And I'm no different. If I carefully consider some of the stuff I come unglued over, I honestly must shake my head. Not to shame myself, but to wake myself up and realize there are legitimate things that warrant my mental energy, but is this situation I'm facing today really one of those things?... There are reasonable things to be angry about today, but not slight inconveniences and little things that bump into my happy. God help me and my kid-placemat life.

Unglued, pages 121, 125

3. Perspective-magnifying experiences are situations that seem impossibly difficult but ultimately reveal the hand of God in action. Recall an experience of provision or deliverance that you attribute directly to God's power. How did this experience of God's goodness change your perspective on the situation? How did it change you?

One way to encourage growth in gentleness is to actually seek out perspective-magnifying opportunities. For example: serving meals in a soup kitchen, volunteering at a nursing home or pediatric cancer ward, tutoring kids at a local elementary school.

What is your initial reaction to this idea—are you more inclined to dismiss it or to seriously consider it? If you were to seriously consider it, what might be your first step?

Guided Prayer

God, thank You for reminding me that Your perspective is always bigger than my own. Every time I get a glimpse of Your perspective, it changes me.

When it comes to perspective and gentleness in my relationships, I especially need Your help with ... because ...

Lord, thank You for Your unfailing gentleness with me, and for the perspective that comes from knowing You are near. Amen.

● DAY 6: **Gentle Noticing**

The personal studies this week provided an opportunity for you to continue taking field notes on your raw emotions and reactions. If you weren't able to make notes during the week, do so now. Use the charts on pages 131–133 to describe two or three raw emotions or reactions you experienced this week. For guidance and examples, see page 25.

1. Briefly review two things: (1) what you wrote on your charts this week (pages 131–133), and (2) what you wrote in response to question 1 from last week's Day 6 study (pages 97–99). What similarities or differences do you notice between last week and this week in the following areas?

   The frequency of my raw emotions/reactions this week compared to last week . . .

   The people who prompt my raw emotions/reactions this week compared to last week. . .

   My physical and emotional state before the events of this week compared to last week . . .

What happened that prompted my raw emotions/reactions this week compared to last week ...

How I reacted this week compared to last week ...

How my reactions were characterized by exploding or stuffing this week compared to last week ...

The words and phrases I used to label myself afterward ...

Additional observations about this week compared to last week . . .

2. How did you experience God at work in you this week? For example: in experiences of grace, gentle chiseling, or imperfect progress?

Guided Prayer

God, thank You for giving me a clear path to follow through the tangled thicket of my raw emotions. Knowing that there are practical steps I can take helps me to feel empowered rather than helpless.

Today, I ask for strength and encouragement. I need Your strength to help me with . . . I need encouragement because . . .

I entrust myself and my imperfect progress to You. Please help me to believe, really believe, that You see something beautiful in me and that all this hard chiseling will reveal it — in my life and in my relationships. Amen.

PERSON	FIELD NOTES ON MY RAW REACTIONS
	1. What was my physical and emotional state before the event?
	2. What happened that prompted my raw reaction?
	3. How did I react?
	4. Was my reaction characterized by exploding or stuffing? Write "E" in the margin for exploding or "S" in the margin for stuffing.
	5. What words or phrases did I use to mentally label myself afterward?

PERSON	FIELD NOTES ON MY RAW REACTIONS
	1. What was my physical and emotional state before the event?
	2. What happened that prompted my raw reaction?
	3. How did I react?
	4. Was my reaction characterized by exploding or stuffing? Write "E" in the margin for exploding or "S" in the margin for stuffing.
	5. What words or phrases did I use to mentally label myself afterward?

PERSON	FIELD NOTES ON MY RAW REACTIONS
	1. What was my physical and emotional state before the event?
	2. What happened that prompted my raw reaction?
	3. How did I react?
	4. Was my reaction characterized by exploding or stuffing? Write "E" in the margin for exploding or "S" in the margin for stuffing.
	5. What words or phrases did I use to mentally label myself afterward?

SESSION

5

Lingering Words
for the Unglued

Group Discussion: *Checking In* (5 MINUTES)

If your group meets for two hours, allow 10 minutes for this discussion.

Welcome to Session 5 of *Unglued*. A key part of getting to know God better is sharing your journey with others. Before watching the video, briefly check in with each other about your experiences since the last session. For example:

- What insights did you discover in the personal study or in the chapters you read from the *Unglued* book?
- How did the last session impact your daily life or your relationship with God?
- What questions would you like to ask the other members of your group?

Video: *Lingering Words for the Unglued* (12 MINUTES)

Play the video segment for Session 5. As you watch, use the outline (pages 135 – 138) to follow along or to take notes on anything that stands out to you.

Notes

Michelangelo's grave is a beautiful picture of words that linger.

What will be my lingering words?

Negative inside chatter: misguided thoughts that can easily turn into perceptions that then turn into dangerous realities.

We assume how we feel about ourselves is how God must see us. What we feel might be true of our current circumstances, but circumstances don't define us.

God has a vision for us beyond the unglued circumstances we find ourselves in.

How the Bible summarizes a life:

Joseph: "The LORD was with Joseph and gave him success in whatever he did" (Genesis 39:23).

David: "God testified concerning him: 'I have found David son of Jesse, a man after my own heart'" (Acts 13:22).

Abraham: Friend of God (James 2:23)

Gideon: Mighty warrior (Judges 6:12)

Joshua: "As for me and my household, we will serve the LORD" (Joshua 24:15).

Job: "There is no one on earth like him; he is blameless and upright, a man who fears God and shuns evil" (Job 1:8).

"Rejoice always, pray continually, give thanks in all circumstances; for this is God's will for you in Christ Jesus" (1 Thessalonians 5:16 – 18).

Three lingering words:

1. Joyful

"Consider it pure joy, my brothers and sisters, whenever you face trials of many kinds" (James 1:2).

I may not always feel the joy, but I can consider where the joy might be.

2. Prayerful

I look for evidence of God's presence all around me. When I connect things that happen in my day to things I've asked God for in prayer, it makes my relationship and my prayer life come alive.

3. Thankful

I don't *have to* do my life; I am *able to* live my life.

I can write these words into the script of my life.

"Finally, brothers and sisters, whatever is true, whatever is noble, whatever is right, whatever is pure, whatever is lovely, whatever is admirable — if anything is excellent or praiseworthy — think about such things. Whatever you have learned or received or heard from me, or seen in me — put it into practice. And the God of peace will be with you" (Philippians 4:8 – 9).

Group Discussion

Video Debrief (5 MINUTES)

If your group meets for two hours, allow 10 minutes for this discussion.

1. What part of the video teaching had the most impact on you?

Word Power (7 MINUTES)

If your group meets for two hours, allow 15 minutes for this discussion.

2. When you have an unglued experience, which of the following behaviors tend to characterize your words? Choose one or two.

- ☐ Exaggerating
- ☐ Yelling
- ☐ Complaining
- ☐ Spinning the truth to make it more presentable
- ☐ Refusal to apologize or acknowledge fault
- ☐ Denying authentic emotion
- ☐ Dominating the conversation

- ☐ Being harsh
- ☐ Self-justifying
- ☐ Belittling someone else's views or experience
- ☐ Sarcasm
- ☐ Interrupting
- ☐ Retaliating
- ☐ Other:

How would you describe the *power dynamic* of these verbal behaviors—on you and on the other person? For example, do they make you feel more in control, help you to feel safe, shut down the other person?

3. Spoken or written, thought or heard, words have power.

   - What is your earliest memory of powerful words? Briefly describe them. For example: were they words you read, heard, or spoke yourself? Were they life-giving or life-taking words?

   - Why have these words lingered with you?

Runaway Words to Lingering Words (26 MINUTES)

If your group meets for two hours, allow 45 minutes for this discussion.

4. Lysa described the damaging power of runaway words—misguided thoughts that lead to flawed perceptions that in turn can become dangerous realities.

   - What runaway words or phrases tend to make up your negative inside chatter? For example: *Loser. Failure. Everyone else is better than you. Why did you just say that? Everyone thinks you're annoying. You're invisible.*

cont.

- Where is this kind of negative inside chatter leading you? In other words, what kind of person could you become if this way of thinking were to continue unchallenged?

5. Instead of allowing runaway words to have power over us, we can empower ourselves with lingering words — words that convey truth. "Think about such things," is how the apostle Paul puts it in Philippians 4:8. Other Bible versions translate this phrase as "fix your thoughts" (NLT) or "keep your minds on" (CEV).

   The Greek word for the verb "think about" is *logizomai* (log-id´-zom-ahee). It means to consider a matter deliberately, draw a logical conclusion, and then make a decision. This kind of thinking is not random pondering but fact-based reasoning. The ancient Greek philosopher Plato used *logizomai* specifically to describe "thought unaffected by the emotions, which seeks to grasp objective facts and apply them."*

   Keeping this understanding in mind, read aloud the apostle Paul's familiar teaching from Philippians:

   > Finally, brothers and sisters, whatever is true, whatever is noble, whatever is right, whatever is pure, whatever is lovely, whatever is admirable — if anything is excellent or praiseworthy — *think about* such things. Whatever you have learned or received or heard from me, or seen in me — put it into practice. And the God of peace will be with you. (Philippians 4:8 – 9, emphasis added)

- Based on this passage, what kind of distinctions might you make between runaway thoughts and lingering words?

---

*Johannes Eichler, "reckon, think, credit," *New International Dictionary of New Testament Theology*, vol. 3, Colin Brown, gen. ed. (Grand Rapids: Zondervan, 1978, 1986), 822 – 823.

- In a sense, Paul is saying something like this: *These are the facts. Do the math, make some decisions, and act on them.* How would you describe the facts and the decisions implied in this passage?

- What do you find especially challenging or encouraging about this teaching when you consider applying it to your experiences of negative inside chatter?

Optional Individual Activity and Group Discussion:
My Lingering Words (23 MINUTES)

If your group meets for two hours, include this activity and discussion as part of your meeting. Allow 23 minutes total — 8 minutes for the individual activity and 15 minutes for the group discussion.

Individual Activity (8 MINUTES)

Complete this activity on your own.

1. Use the Good Words list on page 142 to reflect on the kinds of things you hope might be said about you at the end of your life.
2. Place a checkmark next to any words you strongly hope will be said about you. Draw a line through any words you strongly hope will *not* be said about you (there may or may not be any).
3. Briefly review the words you checked. Circle your top four to six words.

Group Discussion (15 MINUTES)

1. Begin the discussion by simply naming your good words. Without additional comment, go around the group and have each person read aloud the top four to six words circled on the Good Words list.
2. What thoughts or emotions are you aware of in response to hearing all of these good words?
3. What observations do you make about the kinds of words that were chosen by the group overall?
4. Were there any words on the list you crossed out because you did *not* want them to be said about you? If so, what are the words and what makes them objectionable to you?

Good Words

☐ Adventurous	☐ Generous	☐ Playful
☐ Affectionate	☐ Gentle	☐ Prayerful
☐ Beautiful	☐ Good	☐ Pure
☐ Bold	☐ Gracious	☐ Quiet
☐ Brave	☐ Grateful	☐ Quirky
☐ Brilliant	☐ Happy	☐ Rational
☐ Calm	☐ Honest	☐ Reliable
☐ Capable	☐ Hopeful	☐ Respectful
☐ Charismatic	☐ Hospitable	☐ Responsible
☐ Charming	☐ Humble	☐ Risk-taking
☐ Cheerful	☐ Industrious	☐ Secure
☐ Clever	☐ Intelligent	☐ Self-controlled
☐ Compassionate	☐ Interesting	☐ Sensitive
☐ Confident	☐ Joyful	☐ Soulish
☐ Content	☐ Just	☐ Sweet
☐ Courageous	☐ Kind	☐ Tactful
☐ Creative	☐ Knowledgeable	☐ Talented
☐ Curious	☐ Lovely	☐ Teachable
☐ Daring	☐ Loving	☐ Thankful
☐ Dependable	☐ Loyal	☐ Thoughtful
☐ Diligent	☐ Merciful	☐ Trusting
☐ Disciplined	☐ Modest	☐ Trustworthy
☐ Easygoing	☐ Natural	☐ Unswerving
☐ Elegant	☐ Noble	☐ Upbeat
☐ Enthusiastic	☐ Offbeat	☐ Virtuous
☐ Faithful	☐ Optimistic	☐ Whimsical
☐ Fearless	☐ Outspoken	☐ Wise
☐ Forgiving	☐ Passionate	☐ Youthful
☐ Friendly	☐ Patient	☐ Zany
☐ Fun-loving	☐ Peaceful	☐ Zealous
☐ Funny	☐ Persevering	☐ Other:

6. At the end of each session, you've had the opportunity to spend some time talking about your connections within the group, and especially about how to be good companions for one another.

   • What are your observations about this portion of the discussion? For example, what, if any, differences do you notice in yourself and in the group when you are talking about yourself in relationship to the group (rather than about the content of the study or your other relationships)?

- Do you tend to look forward to this portion of the discussion or do you find yourself wishing you could avoid it? Why?

Individual Activity: *What I Want to Remember* (2 MINUTES)

Complete this activity on your own.

1. Briefly review the outline and any notes you took.
2. In the space below, write down the most significant thing you gained in this session — from the teaching, activities, or discussions.

What I want to remember from this session . . .

Closing Prayer

Close your time together with prayer.

Get a Headstart on the Discussion for Session 6

As part of the group discussion for Session 6, you'll have an opportunity to talk about what you've learned and experienced together throughout the *Unglued* study. Between now and your next meeting, take a few moments to review the previous sessions and identify the teaching, discussions, or activities that stand out most to you. Use the worksheet on page 144 to briefly summarize the highlights of what you've learned and experienced.

Session 6 Headstart Worksheet

Take a few moments to briefly summarize what you've learned and experienced throughout the *Unglued* study. You may want to review notes from the video teaching, what you wrote down for "What I Want to Remember" at the end of each group session, responses in the personal studies, field notes, etc. Consider such questions as:

- What struggles or progress did I experience related to this session?
- What was the most important thing I learned about myself in this session?
- How did I experience God's presence or grace related to this session?
- How did this session impact my relationships with the other people in the group?

Session 1: Grace for the Unglued (pages 11 – 39)

Session 2: Freedom for the Unglued (pages 41 – 72)

Session 3: Four Kinds of Unglued (pages 73 – 103)

Session 4: A Procedure Manual for the Unglued (pages 105 – 133)

Session 5: Lingering Words for the Unglued (pages 135 – 164)

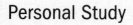

Personal Study

● DAY 1: **Study and Reflect**

Use the charts on pages 162 – 164 to briefly document any observations about your emotions and reactions over the last twenty-four hours (see page 25 for guidance and examples).

> I can decide now what I want to be known for—words that sum up my life, my impact, my influence, my contribution to this world. What will be my lingering words?
>
> *Unglued* DVD

1. Turn to page 141 and, if you haven't already done so, complete the individual activity. Below, write down the four to six words you circled on the Good Words list.

   1.

   2.

   3.

   4.

   5.

   6.

   To better understand what these words represent to you, choose three to consider in greater depth. Write them in the left column of the chart on page 146.

   In the second column, consider the people you know who embody what this word represents. For example, if your word is *brave*, who in your life would you describe as consistently brave? They could be people you know now or people you once knew. For each word, write the names of one or two people who embody this characteristic.

   Use the final column to consider the impact these people have had on you. For example, what have they said or done that leads you to characterize them as brave? How has their bravery influenced you or made a difference in your life?

MY GOOD WORDS	PEOPLE WHO EMBODY THESE WORDS	HOW I HAVE BEEN IMPACTED

2. What insights or encouragements do you gain from connecting your good words to people who embody those words? How does it help you to better understand what it might mean to live out these words in your own life?

Lingering words are words that are true, noble, right, pure, lovely, admirable, excellent, or praiseworthy (Philippians 4:8). Think about such things. Don't get overwhelmed thinking about living these words for the rest of your life. Just think about what words you want to live today, because today is a great day for some intentionally chosen words.

Unglued DVD

3. Choose one of the words from your chart (page 146). Identify two ways you can intentionally live out that word within the next day or two. You may wish to choose one thing that is fairly simple and easy to do and another that is a little bit more of a stretch. Try to choose things that are actionable and specific so you can know for certain whether or not you've done them. If you find it difficult to identify actionable ways of living out your word, consider choosing a different word from your chart.

Guided Prayer

God, thank You for all the good words I have experienced in my relationship with You — mercy, love, forgiveness, hope, joy, and so many more.

Every day, I want my thoughts and my actions to be characterized by good words. The word that stands out most to me from this study is . . . I especially need Your guidance and help to live out this word because . . .

Lord, in all things, at all times, You are always good. I surrender myself to Your care, Your guidance, and Your love. Amen.

● DAY 2: Read and Learn

Use the charts on pages 162 – 164 to briefly document any observations about your emotions and reactions over the last twenty-four hours (see page 25 for guidance and examples).

Read chapter 9 of the *Unglued* book. Use the space below to note any insights or questions you want to bring to the next group session.

● DAY 3: **Study and Reflect**

Use the charts on pages 162 – 164 to briefly document any observations about your emotions and reactions over the last twenty-four hours (see page 25 for guidance and examples).

> The more I compare, the emptier I become. So empty.
>   And empty women, oh how we come unglued.
>   Especially when the empty settles in the part of our souls where unmet desires restlessly wait. And in that dark corner, desperation churns for what could be but isn't, and what we want but still don't have.
>
> *Unglued*, page 132

1. When you consider the season and circumstances of your life right now, which of the desires listed below are you aware of feeling most strongly? Check up to three.

I am most aware of my desire for . . .

☐ *Wholeness*: I want my life to feel complete.

☐ *Contribution*: I want to meet needs and use my life to help people.

☐ *Achievement*: I want to excel and make things happen in life.

☐ *Beauty/meaning*: I want to experience life deeply.

☐ *Understanding*: I want to make sense of life.

☐ *Security*: I want to have certainty in life.

☐ *Joy*: I want to enjoy and celebrate the goodness of life.

☐ *Power/influence*: I want to realize a vision for how life could be different.

☐ *Peace*: I want to experience balance and calm in life.

☐ Other:

Circle one of the desires you checked and use it as your focus for the remainder of the study.

What is it that makes you especially aware of this desire in your life right now?

Within the context you just described, how would you assess the intensity of this desire? Circle the number on the continuum that best describes your response.

1	2	3	4	5	6	7	8	9	10
Mild		**Moderate**		**Strong**		**Very Strong**		**Extreme**	
I am occasionally aware of it.		I am aware of it sometimes more than others.		I am consistently aware of it.		I am almost always aware of it.		I find it difficult to think about anything else.	

2. By God's design, we long for many good things — all of which are meant to draw us back to Him as the source of what we desire. But when the ache of unmet desires intensifies, God's goodness to others can sometimes cause us — knowingly or unknowingly — to doubt His goodness to us. Then we are vulnerable to jealousy and envy.

   Jealousy: a fear of loss of possession or affection; a feeling of hostility toward a rival or one believed to enjoy an advantage

   Envy: a painful or resentful awareness of an advantage enjoyed by another joined with a desire to possess that same advantage

   What are you afraid of losing (or never having) in connection with your desire?

   How does this fear impact your relationship with God or your trust in God's goodness to you?

When you desire something you don't yet have, how do you tend to respond? For example, do you secretly nurse envy and jealousy, share your longings in a vulnerable way, complain about your dissatisfaction? How does this tendency impact your relationships?"

> The best solution I know [to jealousy and envy] ... is pure truth from God's Word ... we need to carry our own load (Galatians 6:4 – 5), and then carry some love to others (Galatians 6:9 – 10).
>
> *Unglued*, page 135

3. In his letter to the church at Galatia, the apostle Paul provides practical teaching about avoiding the kind of comparisons that can lead to jealousy and envy:

   Each one should test their own actions. Then they can take pride in themselves alone, without comparing themselves to someone else, for each one should carry their own load. (Galatians 6:4 – 5)

   For a fresh perspective on this passage, read it again from *The Message*:

   Make a careful exploration of who you are and the work you have been given, and then sink yourself into that. Don't be impressed with yourself. Don't compare yourself with others. Each of you must take responsibility for doing the creative best you can with your own life. (Galatians 6:4 – 5 MSG)

   Paul's first directive is about switching focus — from someone else to ourselves — by engaging in a self-test. The Greek word Paul uses for "test" is *dokimazo* (dok-im-ad´-zo). It is the kind of testing that enables a person to recognize and prove what is good and authentic.[*]

   ---

   [*]Hermann Haarbeck, "test, accept as proved, approve," *New International Dictionary of New Testament Theology*, vol. 3, Colin Brown, gen. ed. (Grand Rapids: Zondervan, 1978, 1986), 808.

Keeping in mind the desire you've identified (page 149), what two or three things would you say are good and authentic about who you are and about your life as it is right now?

What do you think might be your "load" or the "work you have been given" in connection with what is good and authentic about you and your life right now?

How do you understand the idea of doing your "creative best"? In other words, what do you sense might be God's unique invitation to you in your life as it is right now?

4. After teaching that we must first shift our focus from others to ourselves, Paul then shifts the focus back to others just a few verses later. This time, our purpose is not to make comparisons but to carry love:

> Let us not become weary in doing good, for at the proper time we will reap a harvest if we do not give up. Therefore, as we have opportunity, let us do good to all people, especially to those who belong to the family of believers. (Galatians 6:9 – 10)

Comparison always leads to a spiritual dead end — we either feel resentful about our perceived lack or prideful about our perceived superiority. In contrast, carrying love — doing good — is a life-giving path that leads to a spiritual harvest.

In what ways, if any, might your unmet desire (page 149) become a source of love rather than lack—something that energizes you and enables you to carry love to others?

Guided Prayer

God, I am so grateful to be made in Your image—capable of emotions and desires that can draw me closer to You.

Right now, I am aware of my desire for ... This means so much to me because ... I ache for what I don't have, but even more than this, I want to desire more of You. I ask for ...

Lord, above everything else I long for, I want to desire more of You—to prefer nothing in my life to You and Your loving will for me. Amen.

● DAY 4: **Read and Learn**

Use the charts on pages 162–164 to briefly document any observations about your emotions and reactions over the last twenty-four hours (see page 25 for guidance and examples).

Read chapter 10 of the *Unglued* book. Use the space below to note any insights or questions you want to bring to the next group session.

● DAY 5: **Study and Reflect**

Use the charts on pages 162–164 to briefly document any observations about your emotions and reactions over the last twenty-four hours (see page 25 for guidance and examples).

> We engage in inside chatter when we hyper-analyze a conversation after the fact. The back-and-forth in our heads sounds something like this:
>
> *When I said this, she probably thought that.*
> *Now she probably thinks this.*
> *Maybe I should say something to fix it, but then she might think I'm a crazy overanalyzer.*
> *Oh good grief, why did I say that? . . .*
>
> Have you ever been taunted by thoughts like these? I have. Why do we let such destructive words fall hard on our souls? Toxic thoughts are so dangerous because they leave no room for truth to flourish. And lies are what reign in the absence of truth.
>
> *Unglued*, pages 147, 141

1. What kind of back-and-forth inside chatter happens in your head after you have a conversation that prompts you to hyper-analyze what was said?

Do you tend to bring these anxious thoughts into the relationship by asking the other person for clarification, or to keep them to yourself by making assumptions about what the other person is thinking? How does your tendency impact you? How does it typically impact the other person?

2. One of the best strategies for quieting negative inside chatter is immersing ourselves in truth. In his letter to the church at Philippi, the apostle Paul describes a truth-immersion process for keeping our hearts and minds at peace:

> Fix your thoughts on what is *true*, and *honorable*, and *right*, and *pure*, and *lovely*, and *admirable*. Think about things that are *excellent* and *worthy of praise*. Keep putting into practice all you learned and received from me—everything you heard from me and saw me doing. Then the God of peace will be with you. (Philippians 4:8–9 NLT, emphasis added)

The left column of the chart on pages 156–157 includes the eight emphasized words and phrases from the Philippians passage. As you soak in the meaning of these words, use the right column to write down any connections you make between the words and the negative inside chatter you identified in question 1. Connections could include exposing a lie you may have bought into, discovering a new perspective, making a confession, naming what you need from God, or anything else that comes to mind when you consider your inside chatter in light of the words on the chart.

In what ways, if any, does running your inside chatter through Paul's truth-immersion process shift your perspective or move you closer to experiencing peace? If you found that the process wasn't helpful, what makes this issue especially difficult for you?

I CAN FIX MY MIND ON WHAT IS . . .	HOW THIS WORD CONNECTS TO MY NEGATIVE INSIDE CHATTER
True: valid, reliable, honest, sincere, real, faithful, trustworthy	
Honorable: noble, worthy of reverence, holy	
Right: upright, just, worthy of God's approval	
Pure: holy, spotless, uncorrupted, whole	

I CAN FIX MY MIND ON WHAT IS ...	HOW THIS WORD CONNECTS TO MY NEGATIVE INSIDE CHATTER
Lovely: pleasing, agreeable, pleasant, graceful	
Admirable: praiseworthy, attractive, meeting the highest standards	
Excellent: virtuous, good and correct behavior, exhibiting qualities that make up good character	
Worthy of praise: highly regarded, commendable, laudable, exemplary	

> We can foster the honor, encouragement, and love we desire by giving our friends permission to quiet their inside chatter. What does that look like? It might be just a quick phone call to say, "When you and I have had a conversation, you don't ever have to worry about how I'll analyze everything later. I'm not thinking you're crazy or high-maintenance or wacky, okay? I love you. And if I need clarification about something, I'll just call and process it with you." ... Indeed, today is a great day to call a friend and say, "I love you. That's all I'm thinking. Period."
>
> *Unglued*, pages 147–148

3. How do you imagine you might respond if were to give you permission to quiet your inside chatter? For example, would you feel grateful, relieved, awkward, self-conscious?

If you could script the conversation and the setting, what would you hope the other person might say? Where and when would you want them to say it?

Based on what would feel good for you, consider how you might initiate a similar conversation in a relationship where you suspect someone may have negative inside chatter about you or be making assumptions about what you're thinking. If you were to give them permission to quiet their inside chatter, what might you say? When and where could you say it that would help them to feel most at ease?

Guided Prayer

God, thank You for the promise that Your truth leads to peace. I want that peace so much!

   Sometimes my own anxious thoughts take up so much space that they crowd out the truth. I am especially aware of this in my relationship with ... I need Your help to ...

Lord, I surrender myself and my relationships to You. Please quiet my anxious thoughts and help me to rest secure in the peace You give. Amen.

● DAY 6: Gentle Noticing

The personal studies this week provided an opportunity for you to continue taking field notes on your raw emotions and reactions. If you weren't able to make notes during the week, do so now. Use the charts on pages 162 – 164 to describe two or three raw emotions or reactions you experienced this week. For guidance and examples, see page 25.

1. Briefly review two things: (1) what you wrote on your charts this week (pages 162 – 164), and (2) what you wrote in response to question 1 from last week's Day 6 study (pages 128 – 129). What similarities or differences do you notice between last week and this week in the following areas?

    The frequency of my raw emotions/reactions this week compared to last week ...

The people who prompt my raw emotions/reactions this week compared to last week . . .

My physical and emotional state before the events of this week compared to last week . . .

What happened that prompted my raw emotions/reactions this week compared to last week . . .

How I reacted this week compared to last week . . .

How my reactions were characterized by exploding or stuffing this week compared to last week . . .

The words and phrases I used to label myself afterward . . .

Additional observations about this week compared to last week . . .

2. How did you experience God at work in you this week? For example: in experiences of grace, gentle chiseling, or imperfect progress?

Guided Prayer

God, I am so grateful for Your love and for Your patience with my imperfect progress. Some days I feel encouraged and other days it's a struggle to hang on to the hope that I really can change.

Today, I am particularly aware of my need for . . . because . . .

I entrust myself and my imperfect progress to You. Help me to hear Your voice of truth over the noise of my own internal chatter. Lead me straight into the arms of Your peace. Amen.

PERSON	FIELD NOTES ON MY RAW REACTIONS
	1. What was my physical and emotional state before the event?
	2. What happened that prompted my raw reaction?
	3. How did I react?
	4. Was my reaction characterized by exploding or stuffing? Write "E" in the margin for exploding or "S" in the margin for stuffing.
	5. What words or phrases did I use to mentally label myself afterward?

PERSON	FIELD NOTES ON MY RAW REACTIONS
	1. What was my physical and emotional state before the event? 2. What happened that prompted my raw reaction? 3. How did I react? 4. Was my reaction characterized by exploding or stuffing? Write "E" in the margin for exploding or "S" in the margin for stuffing. 5. What words or phrases did I use to mentally label myself afterward?

PERSON	FIELD NOTES ON MY RAW REACTIONS
	1. What was my physical and emotional state before the event?
	2. What happened that prompted my raw reaction?
	3. How did I react?
	4. Was my reaction characterized by exploding or stuffing? Write "E" in the margin for exploding or "S" in the margin for stuffing.
	5. What words or phrases did I use to mentally label myself afterward?

SESSION

6

Imperfect Progress
for the Unglued

Group Discussion: *Checking In* (5 MINUTES)

If your group meets for two hours, allow 10 minutes for this discussion.

Welcome to Session 6 of *Unglued*. A key part of getting to know God better is sharing your journey with others. Before watching the video, briefly check in with each other about your experiences since the last session. For example:

- What insights did you discover in the personal study or in the chapters you read from the *Unglued* book?
- How did the last session impact your daily life or your relationship with God?
- What questions would you like to ask the other members of your group?

Video: *Imperfect Progress for the Unglued* (19 MINUTES)

Play the video segment for Session 6. As you watch, use the outline (pages 165 – 168) to follow along or to take notes on anything that stands out to you.

Notes

To prepare well for our next season, we have to release some things like old habits, old patterns, old ways of thinking.

"Never let loyalty and kindness leave you! Tie them around your neck as a reminder. Write them deep within your heart. Then you will find favor with both God and people, and you will earn a good reputation" (Proverbs 3:3–4 NLT).

"Sow for yourselves righteousness, reap the fruit of unfailing love, and break up your unplowed ground; for it is time to seek the LORD, until he comes and showers righteousness on you" (Hosea 10:12 NIV 1984).

Every choice that honors God bears the fruit of God's unfailing love.

Nothing can separate us from the love of God (Romans 8:38–39).

Don't resist the blessing of brokenness. It tills the ground of your heart.

Choose to see emptiness as the perfect spot for a beautiful space of grace in your life.

When you extend grace, God will open up mercy's storehouse and lavish on you even more grace. His grace never runs out.

I can be patient and I can choose gentleness. I can choose grace. I can choose to embrace change.

Session review:
1. We can declare that we are on God's side.
2. We can trust that God is chiseling us because He sees us as a masterpiece. Let God chisel.
3. We uncovered four different kinds of reactions and set a new goal of soul integrity — honesty that's godly.
4. We developed a procedure manual for our reactions.
5. We can predetermine lingering words — good things to think about instead of negative inside chatter.
6. Change won't be easy, but it is possible.

God longs for you to know real victory over all those unglued moments, not settling for a life that doesn't quite overcome the issues.

God loves you eternally and He's thrown away the key; He will never unlock you from His eternal love.

Take God's hand, release what needs to be released, embrace a new season, trust His love, and walk in the beautiful opportunity for imperfect progress.

The great unglued will still call for us to entertain its wild and unpredictable realities, but you have been made new.

Group Discussion

Video Debrief (5 MINUTES)

If your group meets for two hours, allow 10 minutes for this discussion.

1. What part of the video teaching had the most impact on you?

Seasons of the Soul (7 MINUTES)

If your group meets for two hours, allow 15 minutes for this discussion.

2. At the beginning of the video, Lysa used winter trees to illustrate the importance of being prepared to move forward into the next season of growth. In both nature and life, every season has a unique purpose. Which season would you say best describes where you are right now emotionally and spiritually? Share the reasons for your response.

☐ *Spring*: I am in a season of newness and beauty.

☐ *Summer*: I am in a season of fullness and light.

☐ *Fall*: I am in a season of change and letting go.

☐ *Winter*: I am in a season of darkness and waiting.

☐ *Transition*: I am moving from one season to the next.

Sowing Righteous Relationships (10 MINUTES)

If your group meets for two hours, allow 25 minutes for this discussion.

3. The biblical writers and Jesus Himself often use agricultural metaphors — seasons, soil, planting, seeds, weeds, harvest — to convey spiritual truth. The prophet Hosea uses these earthy images to describe the requirements and benefits of righteousness:

> Plant the good seeds of righteousness, and you will harvest a crop of love. Plow up the hard ground of your hearts, for now is the time to seek the LORD, that he may come and shower righteousness upon you. (Hosea 10:12 NLT)

In this passage, the prophet focuses very specifically on *relational* requirements of righteousness. The command to "plant the good seeds of righteousness" addresses our human relationships. The admonition to "plow up the hard ground of [our] hearts" addresses our relationship with God.[*]

- Based on the passage — especially the metaphors — how would you describe the impact these two kinds of relationships have on each other?

- Which of the two benefits the passage describes — a crop of love and a shower of righteousness — do you feel most in need of right now? Share the reasons for your response.

---

[*]Leon J. Wood, "Hosea," *The Expositor's Bible Commentary*, vol. 7, Frank E. Gaebelein, gen. ed. (Grand Rapids: Zondervan, 1985), 211.

Optional Group Discussion:
Seeds for Right Relationships (23 MINUTES)

If your group meets for two hours, use this discussion as part of your meeting.

1. A seed is an interesting metaphor to use in the context of relationships. Briefly describe what you know about some of the unique characteristics of seeds — where they come from, what they look like, how they work, any experiences you've had with them, etc. What connections do you make between the characteristics of actual seeds and how seeds of righteousness function in a relationship?

2. Go around the group and have a different person read aloud each of the following verses about seeds. As the passages are read, underline any words or phrases that stand out to you. You may wish to read through the list twice to give everyone time to listen and respond.

> Those who plant in tears will harvest with shouts of joy. They weep as they go to plant their seed, but they sing as they return with the harvest. (Psalm 126:5 – 6 NLT)

> Unless a grain of wheat is buried in the ground, dead to the world, it is never any more than a grain of wheat. But if it is buried, it sprouts and reproduces itself many times over. In the same way, anyone who holds on to life just as it is destroys that life. But if you let it go, reckless in your love, you'll have it forever, real and eternal. (John 12:24 – 25 MSG)

> Remember this — a farmer who plants only a few seeds will get a small crop. But the one who plants generously will get a generous crop. (2 Corinthians 9:6 NLT)

> And those who are peacemakers will plant seeds of peace and reap a harvest of righteousness. (James 3:18 NLT)

3. How do the words and phrases you underlined help you better understand your own relationships, or what it means to plant good seeds in your relationships?

4. When you consider the good seeds you have sown in your relationships as part of your imperfect progress, which stage of the growth process best describes those seeds now? For example, are they still hidden beneath the soil, just beginning to sprout up, or producing a bountiful crop? Briefly share any experiences that illustrate your response.

4. Hosea urges God's people "to seek the LORD." Lysa taught that part of seeking the Lord is allowing space in your heart and life for God's grace. She said, "When the circumstances of life just leak you dry, see this emptiness as an opportunity. Instead of reacting out of emptiness, choose to see this emptiness as a beautiful space of grace."

An "opportunity" is not merely one option among many — it is an advantageous chance where conditions are favorable. How do you respond to the idea that the empty or dry places in your life are *opportunities* for grace?

Choosing Imperfect Progress (12 MINUTES)

If your group meets for two hours, allow 25 minutes for this discussion.

5. Change won't be easy, but it is possible. It's a choice — every day we can choose to let God chisel, humbly allowing Him to use the raw material of our lives to craft a masterpiece. And even while God chisels, He affirms the beautiful truth about who we really are — children of the Most High King and dearly loved.

   The psalmist says God "crowns [us] with love and compassion" (Psalm 103:4). A crown is a symbol of royalty. To place a crown on someone is to invest that person with regal dignity and power.

   • What thoughts or emotions are you aware of when you imagine God Himself crowning you, investing you with regal dignity and power?

   • In what ways, if any, does this image shift your perspective or encourage you about your struggles with raw emotions?

6. Briefly discuss what you've learned and experienced together throughout the *Unglued* study.

- What would you say is the most important thing you learned or experienced? How has it impacted you? For example: in your attitudes, behaviors, relationships, etc.?

- How have you recognized God at work in your life through the study—in experiences of grace, imperfect progress, gentle chiseling? What do you sense God's invitation to you might be?

- At the end of every session, you had an opportunity to talk about what you needed from the other members of the group and how you could be good companions for one another. What changes, if any, have you noticed in the ways you interact with each other now compared to the beginning of the study?

Individual Activity: *What I Want to Remember* (2 MINUTES)

Complete this activity on your own.

1. Briefly review the outline and any notes you took.
2. In the space below, write down the most significant thing you gained in this session—from the teaching, activities, or discussions.

   What I want to remember from this session . . .

Closing Prayer

Close your time together with prayer.

Personal Study

● DAY 1: **Read and Learn**

Use the charts on pages 186 – 188 to briefly document any observations about your emotions and reactions over the last twenty-four hours (see page 25 for guidance and examples).

Read chapter 11 of the *Unglued* book. Use the space below to note any insights or questions you want to discuss sometime with a friend or group member.

● DAY 2: **Study and Reflect**

Use the charts on pages 186 – 188 to briefly document any observations about your emotions and reactions over the last twenty-four hours (see page 25 for guidance and examples).

> Where there is a lack of rest, there is an abundance of stress. And where there is an abundance of stress, there is great potential for me to come unglued....
> Sabbath rest has always been part of God's plan for His people.
>
> *Unglued*, page 152

1. Observing the Sabbath includes weekly participation in worship, but biblical Sabbath is about more than going to church. It also includes a commitment to honor God by resting — which can be especially challenging to do in the midst of full and demanding lives. How would you assess your own practice of Sabbath rest right now? Place an ✖ on the continuum to indicate your response.

●————————————————————————————————●

Duty
I do not follow and/or
do not enjoy a practice
of Sabbath rest.

Delight
I consistently follow
and enjoy a life-giving
practice of Sabbath rest.

What words or phrases best characterize your Sabbath observance? (Consider your thoughts and emotions as well as your activities.) Write down four to six words or phrases that come to mind.

Aside from church attendance, would you say that your Sabbath experience is mostly:

☐ *A spiritual asset*—something that consistently helps you to become more like Christ

☐ *A spiritual liability*—something that consistently detracts from your ability to become more like Christ

☐ *Neutral*—neither a spiritual asset nor a spiritual liability

2. The biblical foundation for Sabbath rest begins with God Himself:

> God blessed the seventh day and made it holy, because on it he rested from all the work of creating that he had done. (Genesis 2:3)

The Ten Commandments mandate Sabbath rest (Exodus 20:8 – 10), but God's intention is not that it be a burdensome duty. Instead, God offers Sabbath observance as a gift to His people and intends it to be a source of joy:

> "If you keep your feet from breaking the Sabbath and from doing as you please on my holy day, if you call the Sabbath a delight and the LORD's holy day honorable, and if you honor it by not going your own way and not doing as you please or speaking idle words, then you will find your joy in the LORD, and I will cause you to ride in triumph on the heights of the land and to feast on the inheritance of your father Jacob." For the mouth of the LORD has spoken. (Isaiah 58:13 – 14)

In the Jewish tradition, Sabbath observance—called *Shabbat* in Hebrew—has deep and rich significance. In a Jewish worship book called a *Siddur,* Rabbi Jonathan Sachs describes it this way:

Shabbat is not merely a day of rest, it is a rehearsal, within time, for the age beyond time when humanity, guided by the call of God, moves beyond strife, evil and oppression, to create a world of harmony, respecting the integrity of creation as God's work, and the human person as God's image.*

In other words, Sabbath rest is a rehearsal for heaven — strength training for the weight of glory (2 Corinthians 4:17). Once a week, God invites us to actually *practice* eternity.

Based on the descriptions from Isaiah and the *Siddur*, what do you find most intriguing or inviting about Sabbath?

If this is what I want — to find my joy in the Lord — the Bible makes it clear that rest is key.

I must physically slow down. Stop. Pause. Yes, I am called to rest.

Unglued, page 153

---

3. An observance of Sabbath rest includes both subtractions and additions — we refrain from lesser things in order to make room for greater things. Consider again God's words about observing the Sabbath, this time from *The Message*:

"If you watch your step on the Sabbath and don't use my holy day for personal advantage, if you treat the Sabbath as a day of joy, God's holy day as a celebration, if you honor it by refusing 'business as usual,' making money, running here and there — then you'll be free to enjoy God! Oh, I'll make you ride high and soar above it all. I'll make you feast on the inheritance of your ancestor Jacob." Yes! God says so! (Isaiah 58:13 – 14 MSG)

---

*Rabbi Sir Jonathan Sachs, *The Koren Siddur* (American Edition), (Jerusalem: Koren Publishers, 2009), 325.

Based on the Isaiah passage, which of the "subtractions" it identifies might you find it most difficult to step away from for a day?

What connections, if any, do you make between the subtraction issue you identified and your susceptibility to raw emotions and reactions?

> The more we intentionally practice Sabbath, the more the Sabbath rhythm will become natural to us. Inhale. Exhale. For this is the rhythm of the soul that breathes and lives; it is the rhythm of the soul that doesn't just survive but thrives!
>
> *Unglued*, page 162

4. Jesus strongly challenged religious leaders who adhered to a legalistic Sabbath observance. "The Sabbath was made to meet the needs of people," he said, "and not people to meet the requirements of the Sabbath" (Mark 2:27 NLT).

   What kind of Sabbath would meet your needs right now? What additions and subtractions would help you to routinely experience one day a week as a day of rest, a spiritual asset, and God's gift to you?

Guided Prayer

God, thank You for making rest a good and holy gift. When I am rested — in spirit, mind, and body — everything about my life is better.

Even so, Sabbath rest is a challenge for me. I ask for Your guidance and Your help . . .

Lord, I believe You can give me rest for my soul. I want that so much. In every-thing I say and do, help me to practice eternity now. Amen.

● DAY 3: **Read and Learn**

Use the charts on pages 186 – 188 to briefly document any observations about your emotions and reactions over the last twenty-four hours (see page 25 for guidance and examples).

Read chapter 12 of the *Unglued* book. Use the space below to note any insights or questions you want to discuss sometime with a friend or group member.

● DAY 4: **Study and Reflect**

Use the charts on pages 186 – 188 to briefly document any observations about your emotions and reactions over the last twenty-four hours (see page 25 for guidance and examples).

When I look through the window of my unglued reactions, I may find pride I don't want to acknowledge. Longstanding unforgiveness. Deep-seated bitterness. Simmering anger. Joy-stealing jealousy. Condemning shame. Haunting regrets. Entangling rejection.... Or it could be that I finally acknowledge the very real damage never-ending stresses have caused — that I sometimes both love and despise my life at the same time. And I can't stand that I feel this way. Why do I feel this way?

If things are ever going to get better, we have to acknowledge the underbellies that fuel our unglued reactions. We may not like what we see, but at least we'll know what we're dealing with.

Unglued, page 168

1. Underbellies are vulnerabilities. We protect them and keep them hidden — sometimes even from ourselves — because they expose our weaknesses. In connection with unglued emotions, underbellies are the root causes or underlying issues behind our reactions — things like hurts, disappointments, failures, insecurities, and shortcomings.

As you reflect on the last few weeks of paying attention to your unglued emotions, what underbelly issue(s) have you become increasingly aware of?

In addition to the issues you are aware of, is there anything that has floated around the edges of your awareness — an issue whose importance you have diminished or something you are trying very hard *not* to know about yourself? If so, briefly identify it and note what it is about this issue that makes you want to avoid it.

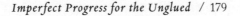

> Might we agree that coming unglued isn't all bad if it brings us to God? And brings to light what's eating away at us in the dark? But even more, might we agree that coming unglued is glorious if the end result of that brokenness leads us to holiness?
>
> *Unglued*, page 169

2. Making wise decisions in the midst of raw emotions is what enables us to move from panic to peace. That transition — and transformation — is holiness in action. At the end of his first letter to the church at Thessalonica, the apostle Paul makes an intriguing connection between peace and holiness:

> Now may the God of peace make you holy in every way, and may your whole spirit and soul and body be kept blameless until our Lord Jesus Christ comes again. God will make this happen, for he who calls you is faithful. (1 Thessalonians 5:23 – 24 NLT)

To make something holy means to bless it, purify it, and set it apart for a divine purpose. The holiness Paul describes is comprehensive — we are to be wholly holy, in every way holy. This holiness encompasses *spirit, soul,* and *body* — the totality of human experience. As you read more about the meaning of each word, use the brokenness you've experienced in your unglued reactions to help you identify what you long for from the God of peace.

- **Spirit (*pneuma*)**: The Greek word *pneuma* can be translated as both *wind* and *spirit*. In this passage, it represents all the ways we encounter God and every aspect of our lives that impacts our oneness with Christ (1 Corinthians 6:17).

What do you long for from the God of peace? How do you want God to bless and purify your spirit?

- **Soul (*psyche*)**: In the New Testament, the Greek word *psyche* can be translated as *heart, mind,* and *soul,* but it is most frequently translated as *life*. We see this usage in familiar passages from the Gospels:

  > Then, turning to his disciples, Jesus said, "That is why I tell you not to worry about everyday [*psyche*] — whether you have enough food to eat or enough clothes to wear. For [*psyche*] is more than food, and your body more than clothing. (Luke 12:22 – 23 NLT)

  > "For whoever wants to save their [*psyche*] will lose it, but whoever loses their [*psyche*] for me and for the gospel will save it." (Mark 8:35)

  Paul uses *psyche* to encompass everything that makes you uniquely *you*. It conveys "the fact of being alive and the aspect of [human existence] which has to do with willing and emotion."*

  What do you long for from the God of peace? How do you want God to bless and purify your soul?

- **Body (*soma*)**: New Testament writers use *soma* in various ways — for example, to refer to a corpse (Matthew 27:52), to the body of Jesus (Mark 15:43), and to physical existence (Mark 5:29). Paul's usage includes the physical, but not as something entirely separate from other aspects of human existence.** For example, in his first letter to the church at Corinth, Paul stresses the intimate connection between the physical and the spiritual:

---

* Colin Brown, "Soul," *New International Dictionary of New Testament Theology*, vol. 3, Colin Brown, gen. ed. (Grand Rapids: Zondervan, 1978, 1986), 684.

** For Paul, "the body is not something external to man which, as it were, is added to his essential self or soul ... *soma* denotes man as a whole, man as a person." Siegfried Wibbing, "body," *New International Dictionary of New Testament Theology*, vol. 1, Colin Brown, gen. ed. (Grand Rapids: Zondervan, 1975, 1986), 234.

> Don't you realize that your [*soma*] is the temple of the Holy Spirit, who lives in you and was given to you by God? (1 Corinthians 6:19 NLT)

Your body is your physical presence on earth and a vehicle for God in this world.

What do you long for from the God of peace? How do you want God to bless and purify your body?

3. If it were up to us, being made whole and holy in spirit, soul, and body would be impossible. But the apostle Paul says it's not up to us: "God will make this happen, for he who calls you is faithful."

   In what ways, if any, have you struggled to believe in God's faithfulness to you in connection with your unglued emotions and reactions, perhaps especially with your underbelly issue(s)?

If you allowed God to make your imperfect progress holy — to bless it and purify it — how do you hope He might use it for a divine purpose?

Guided Prayer

God, thank You for the strong promise that You are faithful and You will make holiness happen in me. That gives me hope!

I want Your peace to lead me through my unglued brokenness and into holiness in every aspect of my life. I am especially aware of my need for Your help with . . .

Your love and grace surround me — spirit, soul, and body. Be my peace in every moment of this day. Amen.

● DAY 5: **Read and Learn**

Use the charts on pages 186 – 188 to briefly document any observations about your emotions and reactions over the last twenty-four hours (see page 25 for guidance and examples).

Read the epilogue of the *Unglued* book. Use the space below to note any insights or questions you want to discuss sometime with a friend or group member.

● DAY 6: **Reflect and Celebrate!**

Congratulations! Having made it this far on your *Unglued* journey, it's virtually guaranteed that you have experienced the *progress* part of imperfect progress. And now it's time to celebrate every forward step.

For this study, instead of reviewing your field notes to compare them with last week, you'll consider your experiences this week in light of the starting point and goal you identified in Session 1 (pages 35 – 36). If you weren't able to make notes during the week, do so now. Use the charts on pages 186 – 188 to describe two or three raw emotions or reactions you experienced this week.

1. Use the left column of the chart (page 184) to write down what you identified in Session 1 as your starting point and goal (questions 2 and 3 on pages 35 – 36). If you weren't able to do this in Session 1, summarize what you can recall about your raw reactions and emotions at that time (starting point) and what you hoped might become your "new normal" (goal).

2. Briefly review your field notes from this week (pages 186 – 188). Use the right column on the chart to first note any differences (small or large) between your experiences this week and what you wrote down as your starting point. Take into account the various factors you've been documenting in your field notes — the frequency of raw emotions/ reactions, people who prompt your reactions, your physical and emotional state, etc. Next, consider these differences in light of your goal. How are you closer to your goal now than you were at the beginning of the course? What steps of progress have you made?

3. As you reflect on the last six sessions, what experiences of God's grace or gentle chiseling stand out most to you as reasons for celebration?

MY STARTING POINT AND GOAL	MY IMPERFECT PROGRESS
My starting point ...	Differences I notice since Session 1...
My goal ...	Steps of progress I have made toward my goal ...

Guided Prayer

God, thank You for Your faithfulness to me! I know that imperfect progress never ends, but I am so grateful for every step You have helped me to take. I especially want to celebrate . . .

I still have work to do — mending relationships, reining in reactions, soaking in truth. I ask for Your strength and guidance in the areas where I am weak and vulnerable . . .

Lord, once again, I entrust my imperfect progress to You. Every step of progress is a sign of Your grace at work in my life. Surround me with grace and more grace in the days ahead. I need You every step of the way. Keep me steadfast in hope, rooted in the promise that I can change because You are faithful. Amen.

PERSON	FIELD NOTES ON MY RAW REACTIONS
	1. What was my physical and emotional state before the event?
	2. What happened that prompted my raw reaction?
	3. How did I react?
	4. Was my reaction characterized by exploding or stuffing? Write "E" in the margin for exploding or "S" in the margin for stuffing.
	5. What words or phrases did I use to mentally label myself afterward?

PERSON	FIELD NOTES ON MY RAW REACTIONS
	1. What was my physical and emotional state before the event? 2. What happened that prompted my raw reaction? 3. How did I react? 4. Was my reaction characterized by exploding or stuffing? Write "E" in the margin for exploding or "S" in the margin for stuffing. 5. What words or phrases did I use to mentally label myself afterward?

PERSON	FIELD NOTES ON MY RAW REACTIONS
	1. What was my physical and emotional state before the event?
	2. What happened that prompted my raw reaction?
	3. How did I react?
	4. Was my reaction characterized by exploding or stuffing? Write "E" in the margin for exploding or "S" in the margin for stuffing.
	5. What words or phrases did I use to mentally label myself afterward?

About Lysa TerKeurst

Lysa TerKeurst is a wife to Art and mom to five priority blessings named Jackson, Mark, Hope, Ashley, and Brooke. The author of more than a dozen books, including the *New York Times*-bestselling *Made to Crave*, she has been featured on *Focus on the Family*, *Good Morning America*, the *Oprah Winfrey Show*, and in *O Magazine*. Her greatest passion is inspiring women to say yes to God and take part in the awesome adventure He has designed every soul to live. While she is the cofounder of Proverbs 31 Ministries, to those who know her best she is simply a carpooling mom who loves her family, loves Jesus passionately, and struggles like the rest of us with laundry, junk drawers, and cellulite.

WEBSITE: If you enjoyed this book by Lysa, you'll love all the additional resources found at *www.Ungluedbook.com*, *www.LysaTerKeurst.com*, and *www.Proverbs31.org*.

BLOG: Dialog with Lysa through her daily blog, see pictures of her family, and follow her speaking schedule. She'd love to meet you at an event in your area! *www.LysaTerKeurst.com*.

A Gift Just for You

Get these free colorful key tags to keep you inspired and on track. Place your order by emailing: resources@Proverbs31.org and reference "Unglued Key Tags" in the subject line. The only charge is $1 to cover shipping and handling. Bulk orders for Bible studies and small groups are also available with special shipping rates.

About Proverbs 31 Ministries

If you were inspired by *Unglued* and desire to deepen your own personal relationship with Jesus Christ, I encourage you to connect with Proverbs 31 Ministries. Proverbs 31 Ministries exists to be a trusted friend who will take you by the hand and walk by your side, leading you one step closer to the heart of God, through:

· *Encouragement for Today,* free online daily devotions

· The *P31 Woman* monthly magazine

· Daily radio programs

For more information about Proverbs 31 Ministries, visit: www.Proverbs31.org

To inquire about having Lysa speak at your event, email: info@lysaterkeurst.com